Aatha and Appachi

Of the People Who Raised Us, and the Way They Never Leave

Valli Saran

Contents

About the Author

Some stories are written.
Some are lived.
And some stay within us
until they find their way onto paper.

This book is not something I simply wrote. It is something I carried — quietly, across decades, through cities and countries, through marriages and grief, through classrooms and chess tournaments and kitchen fires in foreign apartments — until the weight of it finally demanded to be set down in words.

I grew up in a house where wisdom was never announced. It did not arrive with ceremony, did not introduce itself with a clearing of the throat or a gathering of the family. Lessons came wrapped in the ordinary — in the smell of morning coffee, in the way a mistake was received without anger, in the particular silence of two people who had spent a lifetime learning each other. Aatha and Appachi were not my grandparents in the formal sense of the word alone. They were my first landscape. The first world I ever learned to read.

Today, I work as a chess coach, a FIDE Arbiter, School Instructor and a National Instructor with more than a decade of experience working with children. I have sat across tables from hundreds of young minds, watching them struggle and surprise themselves, learning the particular joy of witnessing the moment when something clicks. But long before I ever stood in front of a classroom, I was a child sitting very still, watching two people live — and absorbing, without knowing I was absorbing, everything that would later become the foundation of who I am.

The patience I teach, the discipline I practise, the calm I reach for in difficult moments — none of it originated with me. It began there. In that house. In those early mornings. In the unhurried conversations of two people who never once told me how to live, but showed me, every single day, simply by living it themselves.

This book is my way of holding on to those moments. It is also, I hope, an offering — to a world that is moving faster than ever, that rewards reaction over reflection, noise over stillness, the urgent over the enduring.

If even one person pauses while reading these pages, looks up from the book and thinks of someone who shaped them quietly, someone they perhaps never thanked — then this story has done its purpose. Because in the end, this is not a book only about Aatha and Appachi. It is about the quiet, invisible architecture that certain people build inside us. It is about how the people who raise us continue to live — long after they have gone — in the way we walk through the world.

— Valli Saran

For Aatha and Appachi —

who never taught me life through words,
but through the way they lived it.

Opening Note

There are people who pass through our lives like weather — vivid, disruptive, impossible to ignore. And then there are others whose presence is less like weather and more like atmosphere. You do not notice the air. You simply breathe it. You do not notice the light until the room goes dark. You do not notice the ground until it is no longer beneath you.

Aatha and Appachi were like that for me. They did not perform their love. They did not announce their wisdom. They simply existed — fully, quietly, with a kind of rootedness that I took completely for granted, as children always do with the things that hold them most securely.

I grew up believing that what I had was ordinary. That all mornings began with the aroma of decoction coffee. That all disagreements ended in quiet. That all houses held this particular quality of stillness — not emptiness, but peace. It was only with time and distance, only after I had stepped outside that world and into others, that I began to understand how rare it had been.

This book is not an attempt to sanctify them. They were human beings — with preferences and blind spots, with habits and silences, with their own private griefs I will never fully know. I do not write to make them legendary. I write to remember them as they were: simple, consistent, and quietly extraordinary in that simplicity.

I write because memory, if left unattended, softens and shifts. What stays is often the feeling, the residue — and the feeling, without the detail, is only half the inheritance. I wanted to preserve the detail. The specific weight of a moment at the bank. The exact quality of an evening on the railway platform. The particular way he looked at me when I had done something wrong and chose, instead of scolding, to ask a single question that I am still answering decades later.

These are not grand stories. They are small ones. But I have come to believe that the small stories are the truest ones — that the life of a person is not found in their largest gestures, but in the accumulation of a thousand ordinary moments, each one lived with or without intention, each one leaving its mark.

Because sometimes, the most powerful lives are the ones that never try to be seen.

Chapter – 1 – Before they became Wisdom

Before they became wisdom,
they were simply my world.

There is a particular quality to the homes that shape us — a quality that only becomes visible in retrospect, only after we have moved through enough other houses to understand, by contrast, what we once lived inside. As a child, I could not have articulated it. I only knew, in the wordless way that children know the most important things, that Aatha and Appachi's house felt different. Calmer. Safer. Fuller. As though the walls themselves had absorbed decades of patience and the rooms breathed a little more slowly than rooms elsewhere.

Appachi was tall and lean, carrying himself with an ease that suggested a man entirely at peace with the space he occupied. He did not fill rooms with noise or gesture or the restless energy of a person who needs to be noticed. He filled them with something rarer and harder to name — a quality of presence, a particular stillness that made you feel, simply by being near him, that whatever was happening could be handled. Even in silence, he seemed complete. Even in rest, he seemed purposeful.

Aatha was his opposite and his complement. Where he was still, she moved — with the quick, decisive efficiency of a woman who had arranged the world into order and kept it there by constant, attentive effort. A cotton saree. Hair neatly tied. Hands almost always occupied — with a basket she was weaving, a design she was embroidering, a task she had identified and quietly claimed. She was not restless. There is a crucial difference between restlessness and aliveness, and Aatha possessed only the latter. She moved because the world called for movement. She stopped when stillness was what was needed. She seemed always to know which was required.

The day in that house began before the city woke. Around four in the morning, in the hour that belongs neither to night nor to dawn, when the street outside still lay in the particular hush that precedes the first birdsong, the first sign of life was not movement but aroma. Decoction coffee. It reached you before the sounds did, before any shift in light, drifting through the dark house like an announcement — quiet, certain, unmistakable. It entered the mind before the eyes opened. For years, that smell was my truest alarm clock: not the sharpness of a bell or the intrusion of a voice, but the slow, warm return to consciousness carried on the back of something that meant home.

Aatha moved through the kitchen in those early hours with a care that was almost ceremonial. There was no clatter of urgency, no casual noise of a person simply getting things done. Every movement seemed considered — the vessel lifted with intention, the flame adjusted just so, the rhythm of her work flowing with the quiet precision of someone who had performed these acts ten thousand times and had never once treated them as routine. Even in beginning the day, she protected the sleep of others. Even in her industry, she practiced a kind of courtesy — the courtesy of not disturbing what did not yet need disturbing. That, I came to understand only much later, was itself a form of love. Not the love that announces itself, but the love that acts unseen.

The dawara set, the warmth of the small cup, the concentrated taste of coffee that I would beg for and receive in tiny amounts — these became my earliest rituals of belonging. I would slip from my sleeping place, pad into the kitchen in the half-dark, plead with the particular shamelessness that only small children possess, receive a sip or two, and return to sleep carrying in my chest the warm certainty that I was part of their morning. That I belonged to this quiet world they made before the rest of the world arrived.

After coffee, they would sit together. Not side by side in the manner of two people enduring proximity, but facing each other in genuine conversation — unhurried, unperformed, entirely themselves. They spoke about family and relationships, about the small concerns of daily life and the larger questions of the future. They disagreed sometimes. But even their disagreements had a particular quality — a temperature that never rose to heat, a friction that never became wound. Watching them from the doorway, half-awake, I was witnessing something that I would spend years looking for elsewhere and only occasionally find: friendship living quietly inside a marriage. A partnership so settled in itself that it required no performance, no maintenance of appearance, only the steady continuation of two people genuinely interested in each other's thoughts.

Appachi participated in the household with the same quiet consistency that characterised everything he did. He did not help with the domestic work in the manner of a person granting a favour or making a point. He simply did what needed doing, without announcement and without expectation of acknowledgement, because it was the life they shared and the sharing was complete. There was nothing in his behaviour that suggested he considered any task beneath him. Nothing that distinguished the work of the house from any other serious work. He brought the same attention to all of it.

Aatha's world extended far beyond their house and its rhythms. People came to her — young and old, neighbours and relative strangers — not because she advertised any particular knowledge or authority, but because she possessed something rarer than either: the quality of being genuinely trustworthy. They came with their problems and their confusions, their griefs and their difficult decisions, and she received them all with the same steady attention, the same refusal to rush toward a conclusion. She had an instinct for what each person needed to hear and, perhaps more valuably, for the form in which they needed to hear it. She could give the same understanding in ten different registers — gentle to the gentle, direct to the direct, quietly firm with those who needed a form of firmness they could accept.

In the evenings, she told stories. Small ones, mostly — fragments of her own childhood, episodes from a life that had known both difficulty and grace, observations about people and the patterns of human behaviour that she had accumulated over decades of careful watching. At the time, I received them as entertainment, as the pleasant background music of an evening. I did not understand that I was receiving something far more durable: a way of seeing. A set of lenses, ground to her particular prescription, which I would spend the rest of my life looking through without always realising they had been given to me.

> *As children, we assume that what surrounds us is normal. Only later—often much later— do we understand that we were living inside something rare. Before they became wisdom to me, they were simply life. And that life, without fanfare, without announcement, quietly shaped everything I would become.*

Chapter – 02 – The day He chose silence over scolding

Some lessons don't come as advice.
They come as a single sentence
that you spend the rest of your life unpacking.

There is a category of childhood memory that presents itself, at the time, as entirely unremarkable. Nothing in the moment signals its importance. No music swells. No one announces that what is happening will be remembered. And yet something in the mind recognises — beneath the level of conscious thought — that this moment is different. That it is being filed not in the temporary folder of ordinary days but somewhere deeper, somewhere permanent, to be retrieved years or decades later when its meaning has finally accumulated enough weight to be felt.

I no longer remember the specifics of what I had done. The particular transgression has dissolved with time, leaving behind only its emotional residue — that tightening in the chest, that pre-emptive bracing, the child's practiced calculus of impending consequence. I had done something wrong. I knew it. And I was preparing myself with the particular resignation of a child who has learned to read the weather of the adults around them: the scolding would come, the questions, the rehearsal of the mistake until it had been adequately acknowledged and atoned for.

When Appachi came to know of what I had done, he did not react immediately. There was no hardening of the jaw, no sharp intake of breath, no gathering of the posture into the recognisable shape of parental disappointment. He simply remained himself — quiet, present, occupying the room in the way he always occupied it, as though nothing had shifted in the atmosphere. I watched him. Waited. The waiting, in its way, was its own punishment — not by his design, I think, but simply by the nature of anticipation.

He looked at me. Not with accusation — I have thought about this many times since, the precise quality of that look, and accusation is not the right word. He looked at me with awareness. As though he were seeing me clearly, in full, without the distortion that anger or disappointment introduces. I felt seen. But I did not feel reduced. I was not, in that moment, merely my mistake.

I waited for the questions. They never came. Instead, after a silence that seemed to consider many things before settling on this one, he asked me a single sentence:

"Are you going to wait for decades?"

That was all. No lecture followed. No repetition, no elaboration, no insistence that I explain myself or articulate my understanding of what I had done wrong. The question landed, and then there was only quiet. The conversation, such as it was, ended there. And from that day forward, the mistake was never made again.

The house remained the same. Their behaviour toward me did not alter. There was no prolonged atmosphere of disappointment, no cooling of the warmth with which they held me. The incident was over — truly over — in the way that things in that house were over when they were over. What had shifted was entirely internal. Not from fear of future punishment, not from the vigilance of a child who has learned to watch for danger, but from something more durable: a changed understanding. A new relationship with the concept of consequence. A quiet, privately undertaken responsibility.

Years later, turning that question over again as I have turned it over many times, I understood what he had been asking. A mistake is made in a moment — in a second of inattention or poor judgment or simple human error. But reputation, character, the long slow construction of a life that others trust and respect — that is the work of years.

Sometimes decades. The question was not rhetorical. It was a window, and through it I was meant to see the true distance between who I was in that moment and who I was capable of becoming.

Later in life, I saw its truth confirmed again and again. I saw how quickly people judge and how slowly they revise their judgments. I saw how a single action can calcify into a permanent definition in the minds of others, and how long, how patiently, one must work to offer them a different and truer story. Every time I encountered this — and I have encountered it often — his words returned. Not as a haunting but as a compass. A quiet recalibration.

Around this same period, I witnessed something that would leave its own permanent mark, though I was not even a participant in it. I had come home from playing outside, eaten lunch with Aatha, and drifted into the half-world between wakefulness and sleep, stretched out in the afternoon heat with the television providing its low background murmur.

In that suspended state, I became aware of voices. One was Aatha's — steady, unhurried, entirely herself. The other belonged to a friend of hers, a woman whose voice carried the particular rawness of someone in genuine distress. She was speaking about what others had been saying — unkind things, said behind her back, which she had somehow come to hear and which had lodged themselves in her like splinters, too small to remove, too irritating to ignore. She was replaying the words, turning them over, trying to understand what she had done to deserve them.

Aatha listened without interrupting. This was characteristic of her — this capacity to receive another person's distress without immediately trying to resolve it, to allow it to be fully spoken before she offered any response. When she finally spoke, it was not with consolation or indignation on her friend's behalf. It was with something more useful: clarity.

> *"If a saree falls on a thorn, the loss is to the saree. It must be removed carefully."*

I lay still and heard this and, even in my half-sleep, felt something in the image snap into focus. She was not talking about fabric or thorns. She was talking about the nature of certain kinds of harm — the kind that comes from careless words wielded by people who have not bothered to consider the weight of what they are saying. She was talking about how to respond to such harm, or rather how not to respond: not with answering sharpness, not with the urgency of someone who feels they must defend themselves immediately, but with the patience of someone who understands that the first priority is to remove the thorn without tearing the saree further.

Some situations do not require reaction. They require patience, distance, the quiet skill of extraction. Sometimes protecting yourself is more important — and more difficult — than proving a point. The person who has said unkind things has already shown you something about themselves. You do not owe them the additional gift of your distress.

Neither of them ever forced these understandings upon me. They said what needed to be said, once, in the moment when it needed to be said — and then they simply continued living in accordance with it. That consistency between word and life was what gave their words their particular staying power. Wisdom that is lived does not need to be repeated. It is already everywhere you look.

> *Their wisdom was never loud. It did not perform itself or demand that you notice it. It worked quietly, slowly, like water finding its level — and it is still working in me, still shaping the way I move through the world, decades after it was first given.*

Chapter – 03 – The morning that taught me love

They didn't show love.
They lived it —
in silence, in routine,
in the small, repeated gestures
of a life shared completely.

There are forms of love that announce themselves loudly — that arrive with declarations and demonstrations, with the theatrical gestures by which people communicate, to themselves and to others, the depth of what they feel. And then there are forms of love that never announce themselves at all. That exist not as performance but as constant, underlying presence — as unremarkable and as essential as the structure of a house. You do not think about the walls. You simply live within them.

Aatha and Appachi did not belong to the first category. There were no grand gestures between them, no visible displays of the kind that make bystanders uncomfortable with their own witness. Their affection was not performed for an audience. It did not require one. It was simply the texture of the life they shared — something steady, something deeply settled, something that had long since ceased to need proving because it had become, through years and accumulation, simply fact.

What struck me, in the years when I was old enough to observe but not yet old enough to understand what I was observing, was a quality of genuine interest. They were interested in each other. After decades of shared life, after children and grandchildren and the full accumulation of ordinary existence, they remained — in some essential way that I recognised without being able to name — curious about each other. The morning conversations were not the recitations of couples who have run out of things to discover and now merely exchange information. They were alive. Two people genuinely engaged in the perpetually unfinished project of understanding another human being.

They spoke about everything and nothing. Family, children, grandchildren. The small events of yesterday and the imagined shapes of tomorrow. A piece of news one of them had read. A memory that had surfaced without warning. A question about a neighbour, an observation about the season, a plan that might or might not come to anything. The content mattered less than the quality of attention they brought to it — the tone that was, always, calm and respectful, unhurried, entirely free from the particular weariness that can settle over long marriages when the people inside them have stopped being curious about the distance between them.

Even when they disagreed — and they did disagree, they were two distinct human beings with distinct views on the world — the disagreement never broke the peace of the house. I witnessed no raised voices, no wounded silences, no doors closed with the communicative force of a person who needs to be heard but has given up on words. When they differed, there was a pause. A look. And in that pause and that look, something was worked out between them — some private negotiation conducted in the language of people who have had long enough together to have developed their own vocabulary of gesture and expression. Then the conversation continued. The house remained whole.

Books were a shared world between them. Appachi read widely — English and Tamil, newspapers and novels, history and philosophy — and Aatha read with equal appetite, though her reading ranged toward different territories. They discussed what they had read with the same quality of genuine engagement that characterised all their conversations. They shared their thoughts. They pushed back on each other's interpretations. They disagreed about books with the same calm willingness with which they disagreed about everything else, and neither of them seemed to require agreement as the price of continued respect.

Occasionally, they would draw me into this world. "Read aloud," one of them would say, handing me a page or a passage. I obliged, assuming I was providing them with some service they required. It was only later that I understood: the reading aloud was not for their benefit. It was an invitation. A subtle, unhurried act of inclusion. They were opening a door and letting me walk through it, into the habit of reading not as duty or assignment but as one of the genuine pleasures of a life well-arranged.

One day, all three of us read the same passage and I waited, with the confident certainty of a child who has not yet learned the complexity of truth, for one of them to declare the correct interpretation. The right answer. The way things were. Instead, Appachi looked at me with an expression I have spent years trying to describe accurately, and said that all three of us were right.

I pressed him. This did not seem possible. He explained, patiently, that truth is not a single fixed point but a landscape — that where you stand determines what you see, and that different standpoints yield different but equally genuine understandings. That life becomes more navigable, not less, when you accept that your view is never the only view, and that other people's readings of the same passage, the same experience, the same moment, are not errors but offerings. Aatha added, quietly, that what we believe to be right is most often our assumption — shaped by our history, our character, the particular way our experience has taught us to see — and that holding this truth lightly, with humility, is one of the skills that determines whether a person moves through life in openness or in the constant friction of someone who needs the world to confirm their existing understanding of it.

I did not yet have the vocabulary for what I was receiving. But something in me received it nonetheless.

> *Not everyone can sit in silence with another person and feel complete. Not everyone can disagree and remain connected. What they had was not merely love in the romantic sense of the word — it was understanding, acceptance, and a respect so deep and so habituated that it had become invisible, the*

way air is invisible, the way the ground beneath your feet is invisible until it is no longer there.

If love means speaking softly, honouring difference, protecting one another's dignity in the ten thousand small moments where it would be easier not to — then I learned what love looks like long before I ever had a word for it. I learned it in those mornings, in that kitchen smell, in those unhurried conversations between two people who had decided, somewhere along the way, to keep choosing each other.

Chapter – 04 – What Aatha knew without schooling

Education teaches knowledge.
Life teaches wisdom.
She had the second kind
in everything she touched.

There is a form of intelligence that does not show up in certificates or examinations, that cannot be tested in the conventional sense, that leaves no formal record of itself — and yet produces, in the person who possesses it, a quality of life so ordered and grounded and genuinely useful that you recognise its authority the moment you encounter it. Aatha had this intelligence in abundance. She had it, I came to understand, in the way certain craftspeople have their skill — not learned from a text but accumulated through the attentive practice of living, through the specific, unrepeatable education of paying close attention to the world and to the people in it.

When I think of my childhood in that house, I do not reach first for abstract lessons or moral declarations. I reach for mornings. The particular quality of school-day mornings in the nineties — the half-sleep and mild chaos, the uniform that needed to be found, the school bus that would not wait. Breakfast appeared without my having considered how: idli soft and steaming, chutney fragrant beside it, or sambar that had been simmering since before I woke. Lunch was packed with the same quiet efficiency — curd rice, paruppu saadham, potato fry, a bottle of water that always seemed cooler than water should reasonably be. And then I would rush out, and return later, and leave things scattered as though a small natural disaster had occurred, and behind me, without complaint, Aatha would restore the order I had carelessly undone.

She never reproached me for this in the sharp register of adult frustration. She had the patience — or perhaps the wisdom — to understand that children must be invited into order, not commanded into it. One day she simply asked me to help. Not with the tone of someone assigning a task but with the ease of someone extending a small and pleasant invitation: "Come, let's keep things properly."

I asked why. The question was genuine — I did not yet understand the relationship between the arrangement of physical space and the state of one's inner life. Her answer was simple and precise:

> *"It is not only about neatness. When things are not in place, tension increases. When things are organised, you don't lose time. You don't lose peace."*

At the age I was then, I received this as a mild inconvenience disguised as a life lesson. I wanted to play. What did tidying have to do with playing? Everything, it turned out. When the house moved to her order, when things were where they were meant to be, the hours had a different quality. There was more time, not less. The mental energy that would otherwise be spent in the low-grade, constant friction of things misplaced and searches conducted and small frustrations accumulating into something larger — all of that was freed. I had more time to play, precisely because she had taught me to maintain the conditions that made playing possible.

In those days, children carried their lunches to school in wire baskets — practical, beautiful objects that many families made at home. Aatha made them with a skill accumulated over years, her hands moving with the quick, sure confidence of someone who has performed a craft long enough that the craft has become part of how they think. She involved us in this making not by assigning us the role of assistants but by the simple and effective act of sitting down beside us and beginning. "Let's do it," she would say — and suddenly we were already doing it, already part of something, before we had had time to decide whether we wanted to be.

My first attempts were deeply imperfect. Uneven weave, loose corners, the whole thing slightly lopsided in a way that suggested function without quite achieving it. She never stopped me to correct the error before it had been fully made. She watched, and when the moment was right, she guided with a light hand: "Hold it like this. Not so tight. Let it breathe." The corrections were adjustments rather than criticisms. They treated the mistake not as a failure but as a natural station on the way toward understanding.

One day, we carried those baskets to school ourselves — not because we had been asked to, but because we had made them with our own hands, and this gave them a quality that no purchased object could possess. Pride of authorship. The particular, uncomplicated satisfaction of having made something real in the world.

She taught drawing and embroidery in the same spirit — not as subjects to be studied but as shared moments, as things done together that happened also to result in the acquisition of skill. When we helped, she would say, with a directness that was also a form of generosity: "With your help, I finished it easily." This small acknowledgement, so simply offered, had a disproportionate effect. We wanted to help again, not because we had been instructed to want it, but because helping had been experienced as something meaningful, something that mattered to a person we loved.

I asked her once why Appachi did not practice these domestic skills with the same fluency she possessed. She smiled — the particular smile of a woman who has thought carefully about things and is prepared to share her conclusions:

> *"If something is not practiced early, it will not come easily later. Learning will never spoil you. One day, it will help you be independent."*

She shared, sometimes in those domestic hours, fragments of her own story — her childhood, the difficulties she had navigated, the circumstances that had required her to develop exactly the qualities she was now quietly passing to us. She never framed these stories as cautionary tales or moral illustrations. They were simply her experience, offered with the casual generosity of someone who has made peace with all of it and now considers it simply part of who they are.

> *She had never been to a university. She held no degree that a wall could display. But she possessed*

a form of education that formal schooling only rarely produces: an understanding of the practical, emotional, and relational architecture of a life. She knew how to live. She knew, more precisely, how to help other people learn to live. And she transmitted this not through declaration but through demonstration — not through telling but through the patient, daily act of being exactly who she was, and allowing those near her to watch.

Chapter – 05 – The way She handled people

She didn't avoid people.
She handled them with care —
the way a surgeon handles
something delicate and living.

Some lessons are given to you directly. Someone sits you down, looks you in the eye, and says: here is how this works. This is what I have learned. Take it. These lessons are valuable, but they are also the easiest kind to forget — received formally, stored in the part of memory reserved for things that have been deliberately learned, and therefore subject to all the erosion that deliberately learned things suffer when life fails to call them up.

And then there are the other kind: the lessons that arrive through the side door, when you are not prepared, when you are not even in the room. The lessons you receive by accident, by proximity, by being in the wrong place and at the right time. These are the ones that settle deepest, because they arrive not in the register of instruction but in the register of experience, and the mind holds experience differently than it holds information.

Aatha handled people — all kinds of people, in all kinds of conditions — with a consistency of manner that I noticed long before I understood it. She was not the same with everyone in the sense of delivering the same response regardless of context. She was finely calibrated. She seemed to read, almost immediately upon encountering a person, what they needed from her — not what they were asking for, which is rarely the same thing, but what they actually needed — and she adjusted herself accordingly. With some people she was open and warm and freely expressive. With others she maintained a gentle, slightly more formal distance. But the respect was equal. The regard was equal. Only the register changed.

I puzzled over this distance for a long time. It seemed, from the outside, to contradict the warmth that I knew her to possess. Why would someone capable of such genuine openness choose to hold certain people at arm's length? The question stayed with me until the afternoon I found, almost by accident, the beginning of its answer.

I had come home from a long afternoon of playing and had eaten lunch and stretched out in that pleasant post-lunch heaviness, the television making its low background noise, consciousness drifting pleasantly toward the border of sleep. The voices that reached me through this half-conscious state were, at first, simply part of the ambient sound of the house. Then they resolved into meaning. One voice was Aatha's — calm and level as always, carrying that quality of complete stillness that she brought to every difficult conversation. The other belonged to a friend, and this voice was not calm. It was shaken, tearful, carrying the specific rawness of someone who has been hurt and cannot stop returning to the place of the hurt.

The woman was speaking about what others had been saying about her — unkind things, spoken in her absence, which had somehow found their way back to her. She was carrying it with the exhausting fidelity of a person who replays injury, who cannot set it down because setting it down feels somehow like accepting it. Again and again, she returned to the words. What had she done? Why would they say this? Did it mean something was fundamentally wrong with her?

Aatha listened without interruption for a long time. Then she spoke, and what she said was simple enough to sound modest, but carried the full weight of something that had been lived rather than merely thought:

"Why are you giving weight to people who don't even have the courage to face you? They speak in your absence because they cannot speak to your face. That tells you everything about the value of what they've said. If what you are doing is right — if it lets you sleep at night without shame — then that is your answer. The rest is noise. Don't carry it. Don't give it a room inside you that it hasn't earned."

The conversation ended with the friend calmer, lighter, as though something that had been pressing on her chest had been gently but firmly removed. I lay still and listened to this, in my half-sleep, and filed it somewhere that turned out to be permanent.

Later, when I raised the question of her careful distances — why she kept certain people at a particular remove — she answered without defensiveness or apology, with the same directness she brought to everything:

"It's not that I don't like them. I keep distance so they don't get hurt, and I don't get disturbed. Too much closeness, in the wrong kind of relationship, creates misunderstanding. It creates obligations that neither person is equipped to honour. It introduces a friction

that ends up hurting both people more than the distance ever would."

She was describing, I came to understand, a form of social intelligence that most people develop partially and imprecisely, through the accumulated bruises of relationships that have gone wrong and the gradual, painful recognition of patterns. She had arrived at it not through caution or withdrawal but through observation. She had watched people closely enough, for long enough, to understand the difference between closeness that nourishes and closeness that depletes — and she had organised her life accordingly.

> *Aatha never gossiped. In all my years of watching her, I never heard her speak of absent people with cruelty or diminishment. She never carried the negativity of others as her own burden. She moved forward — always forward, steadily, without the weight of accumulated grievances. At the time, I thought this was patience. Now I understand that it was something more precise than patience. It was clarity. A clear-eyed understanding of where her energy was best spent, and the discipline to spend it there.*

Anyone can react. Reaction is the easiest thing in the world — it requires no skill, no self-possession, no delay between feeling and expression. But to remain calm in the face of provocation, to receive an unfair word without immediately returning it, to choose the considered response over the instinctive one — this is a genuine achievement. She made it look effortless, the way all genuine mastery looks effortless from the outside. It was not effortless. It was the result of a life spent practicing, in the quiet daily laboratory of human interaction, the discipline of not letting the world make your choices for you.

Chapter – 06 – The life She prepared me for

She did not prepare me for the life I had.
She prepared me for the life I didn't yet know was coming.

There is a particular kind of preparation that is invisible while it is happening. It does not announce itself as preparation. It does not feel like training. It feels, at the time, like ordinary life — like helping with tasks that are simply part of the shared work of a household, like acquiring small skills that seem to have no particular destination, like absorbing attitudes and habits that appear to be nothing more than the texture of the people around you. And then one day you find yourself in a new place, with new demands, and you reach for something you need — some skill, some patience, some internal resource — and it is there, already formed, already yours. And you understand, with a start, that someone put it there. Someone was preparing you all along.

Marriage did not transform everything in a single moment. Change of the meaningful kind rarely does. But it introduced new demands with a quiet insistence — a new place, a new routine, a new role, new expectations both stated and unstated, new forms of love that required new forms of capability. In the first weeks, I moved through it all with a sense of excitement that had not yet encountered the full weight of what was required. The excitement was real. The hope was real. But underneath it, in the moments of quieter honesty, was a question: could I actually do this?

The answer, I discovered, was that I could — but not yet in all the ways that would eventually be required. The first morning I stood alone in my new kitchen with the clear intention of cooking something, I chose oatmeal. I chose it for its simplicity, its apparent friendliness toward beginners. Water. Oats. Heat. How difficult could it be? I turned on the stove, added the water, added the oats, and stood back to wait with the confidence of someone who has watched a thing done many times and has mistaken watching for knowing.

A few minutes later, the smell changed. It acquired a note that had no business being in a breakfast — something darker, something wrong. I moved closer. The bottom of the pot had begun to stick, and was now moving through sticking toward burning with a speed that outpaced my capacity to intervene. I tried to salvage it. I could not. The oatmeal had made its position clear. I stood in the kitchen in the aftermath of this small domestic failure and felt, with a disproportionate vividness, the gap between who I thought I was and who the situation required me to be.

I called Aatha. Her voice came through the phone with its characteristic quality of knowing exactly what was needed — not fuss, not drama, not the consolation that would have felt condescending in that moment. Simply: "It's okay. Tomorrow, we will do it together." The word together crossed the distance between us in a way that surprised me with its efficacy. The situation had not changed. The burned oatmeal was still there. But the isolation of the moment dissolved.

The next morning, the kitchen became a classroom, conducted over the phone with Aatha at its head. She walked me through each step — the proportion of water to oats, the temperature, the need for attention, the signs that things were moving in the right direction or the wrong one. I made mistakes. Different mistakes than the day before, new mistakes, the specific mistakes of someone who has been told the right way and has not yet fully internalised it. She corrected each one without impatience, without repeating herself more than necessary, without the faint but unmistakable discouragement that can attach itself to being corrected too many times. She simply continued. The lesson continued. And slowly, over days and weeks, the kitchen began to yield.

The day the dish came out right — not perfect, but genuinely right, recognisably what it was meant to be — I felt something that surprised me with its intensity. Not pride exactly, though pride was part of it. Something more fundamental: the specific satisfaction of competence earned. Of having moved through failure toward capability by the direct route of repeated effort. It felt like a small territory newly claimed.

Looking back at this, I can see what I could not see while it was happening: she had been trying to give me this all along. The wire baskets. The morning organisation. The cooking lessons that I had half-attended and half-resisted because they had seemed, at the time, like the concerns of an older generation rather than the essential skills of an independent life. She had known, with the forward-looking clarity of someone who loves a person and thinks about who they will need to become, that the day would arrive when I would be alone in a kitchen with a pot and a question and no one to answer it. She had been preparing me for exactly that day. I had been too busy to notice.

In the years that followed, I was also navigating a different kind of territory: the path of someone who had entered a field — competitive chess — that her family had not previously occupied, and who was building her own professional identity in it. This required a particular kind of courage that I did not always feel but had learned to perform convincingly enough that it eventually became genuine. Recognition did not come early. The early years contained more doubt than celebration. But she had taught me something about this too, though not explicitly: that work is not merely instrumental, not merely the mechanism by which money is obtained. Work is the form through which self-respect is continually renewed.

> *"Knowledge stays with you," she had said, more than once, in more than one context. "It grows. No one can take it away from you." I had heard this without fully understanding it then. I understand it now. She was describing the one possession that is immune to circumstance, the one investment that compounds without risk.*

I completed my master's degree. I earned my certifications in chess. I built, piece by piece, an identity that was mine — not inherited, not assumed, but constructed through effort and choice and the willingness to keep going past the point where giving up would have been entirely understandable.

The ability to restart — to break, to acknowledge the break, to begin again without requiring that the second beginning be free of the memory of the first failure — this became one of the most reliable tools I carry. I did not arrive at it through some natural resilience. I arrived at it because she had spent years, without ever naming what she was doing, building it in me.

Chapter – 07 – The things that stayed after I left

There is a moment
when you stop living inside a home
and start carrying it within you.
It does not happen all at once.

Distance, when it comes suddenly and completely, has a way of clarifying things that proximity had kept comfortable and unexamined. You do not notice the weight of what you have been given until you lift it and carry it to a new place. You do not understand the shape of the formation you grew inside until you are standing outside of it, looking back, seeing for the first time its outlines.

Moving to a new country is many things at once. It is genuinely exciting — the newness, the expansion, the discovery that the world is larger and stranger and more various than any one life has room to contain. It is also, in ways that take longer to admit, a form of solitude that no amount of modern connectivity entirely resolves. The people who know you most completely are not in the same timezone. The comforts that are most essential — not material comforts, but the particular comfort of being understood without having to explain yourself, of being loved in the specific, personalised way that only comes from long acquaintance — these do not travel well. They do not translate. They exist in a geography, and when you leave that geography, you carry only an echo of them.

Loneliness arrived with a quietness that surprised me. Not the dramatic loneliness of someone who is entirely alone, but the subtler loneliness of someone who is surrounded by people and still misses a particular kind of presence. The presence of people who have known you since before you knew yourself. The presence of a language — not a spoken language, but a relational one — in which everything does not need to be explained from the beginning.

And yet. And yet I found, in that distance, that I was not as unequipped as the newness of the situation sometimes suggested. There were skills I had absorbed without cataloguing them. There were attitudes toward difficulty — a particular patience with the learning curve, a willingness to be imperfect in the process of becoming competent — that turned out to be more portable than I had known. They had been packed inside me, quietly and without my awareness, by two people who had understood, better than I did, what the road ahead would require.

Somewhere in the middle of those early years abroad, I found myself in a cookery competition. Not through any grand ambition, but through the ordinary accumulation of kitchen hours, the practice that had begun with a burned pot of oatmeal and an overseas phone call and had grown, through Aatha's patient instruction and my own stubborn repetition, into something resembling genuine skill. I prepared orange pulav with paneer polichadu. I came first.

The moment mattered to me in a way that was disproportionate to its external significance, and I have thought about why. It was not the award itself. It was the line that connected that moment to a different one — to Appachi's voice, somewhere in memory, saying with quiet certainty: "My child will learn." He had been right. She had been right. I had not always believed them, and they had believed it anyway, and in believing it, they had made it a little more possible.

Then came a morning that was entirely ordinary until it wasn't. The previous evening had been exactly the kind of evening that life produces in abundance when things are going well — dinner with my husband, a film, laughter, the easy contentment of two people who have built something together and are, in that particular moment, aware of having done so. We had returned home late. I had fallen asleep with the uncomplicated completeness of a person who has nothing weighing on them.

The call came in the morning. My in-laws. The quality of their voice was different before any specific words had arrived — a frequency that the body recognises before the mind does, that sends a signal upward through the nervous system with a kind of terrible efficiency. And then the words came. Aatha was gone.

I checked my phone. Missed calls, many of them. Messages accumulating over hours while I had been sleeping beside a good evening. The world had changed while I was not watching. That is how it always is, of course — the world changes while we are not watching, while we are sleeping, while we are laughing at a film — but you never fully believe it until it happens to you.

What I felt in that moment was not the clean, comprehensible shape of grief that we imagine in advance. It was disorientation. A kind of radical unreality, as though the world had been rearranged in the night into a configuration that did not correspond to any map I possessed. The most immediate and vivid thought was not of her — not yet. It was of Appachi. After all those mornings, all those years, all that daily, uninterrupted life of two people who had woven themselves so thoroughly into each other's days that the absence of one would alter the entire fabric — how would he be? What does a person do with a morning when the person who made the mornings meaningful is no longer in them?

For two days I moved through the altered world with tears that came and went like weather. Then, gradually, something else emerged from underneath the grief — something that I recognised, with some surprise, as steadiness. A capacity to continue. Not to be unaffected, but to function alongside the affect, to hold both the pain and the necessary competence of getting through each hour.

I had not manufactured this steadiness in those two days. It had been there already, waiting — built into me over years by two people who had understood, without ever saying so explicitly, that life would require this of me. That the world would deal its blows, and that what would determine the quality of what remained would not be the absence of pain but the presence of resources deep enough to hold it.

She was not there — and yet she was not absent. Because everything around me still carried her. The way I thought about difficulty. The way I reached, automatically, for patience rather than panic. The way I moved toward the people who needed me rather than retreating into myself. That was her. That had always been her. Distance had not diminished it. Time had not eroded it. Even her death had not removed it, because she had not placed these things outside me, where they could be lost. She had placed them inside me, where they could not.

Chapter – 08 – The words I could not hear again

Some goodbyes are never spoken.
They exist only as absences —
places where a voice used to be
and now is not.

The flight home felt like time moving at the wrong speed. Not slowly, exactly, but with a different quality of duration — the hours passing with a heaviness that made each one felt, that refused to allow the merciful unconsciousness of ordinary travel. I sat at the window and looked at clouds and did not see them. I thought about arrivals. About the house that was waiting. About who would be in it and who would not.

I had travelled this route many times before, returning from the life I had built abroad to the one I came from, and those returns had always had a particular flavour — anticipation, the mild pleasant exertion of re-entry, the small recalibrations of resuming a language and a rhythm that are yours but not your daily. This time, none of that. This time, the returning was entirely different in quality from anything that had preceded it. I was going back to a house that would be full of people and would still, in the essential way, feel empty.

When I landed, the city received me without ceremony. The airport was the same airport. The roads were the same roads. The air smelled of the same specific mixture of heat and diesel and the particular vegetable green of a city that is always, somewhere, being cultivated. Everything was familiar and nothing was quite right. That is the particular experience of grief in the first days — the world persisting in its ordinary appearance while something fundamental within you has shifted, so that you move through familiar spaces feeling like a visitor.

I had not told many people I was coming. The arrival at the house was quiet — or as quiet as a house full of gathered family can be. People were everywhere, in the particular congregation that death produces, drawn from their scattered lives to this one place by the gravity of loss. I moved through them, receiving their embraces, responding to their words, in the half-present way of someone who is also doing a great deal of interior work simultaneously.

The specific grief of having missed the final goodbye settled in me like a stone. No video call in those last days. No farewell whose weight I had known in advance and prepared for. No last chance to say, directly and with the full intention of saying it: I love you. I see everything you gave me. I understand, now, what you meant. Some goodbyes are never spoken, because we do not know they are goodbyes until after they have already passed, and what remains is only the space where they should have been.

Appachi was standing by his cupboard when I came into the room — doing something ordinary, some small domestic task, a man going about the business of the morning as though mornings still had the same content they always had. The composure of it stopped me. I walked toward him slowly. There seemed to be no hurry. The distance between us was small and I crossed it carefully, as though the floor might give way.

I called his name. Softly. My voice arrived with more tremble in it than I had intended.

"Appachi..."

He turned. Our eyes met. What passed between us in that moment has no adequate language — no clean translation into words that were not the look itself. His eyes confirmed what I already knew: she was gone. But they also said, with equal clarity, the other thing: I am here. You are not alone in this. We will carry it together.

Something broke in me in that moment — not catastrophically, not in the way of things that shatter beyond repair, but in the way that a pressure releases when it has been held too long, when the containing of it has cost more than the releasing will. Tears came without sound. Just the tears and the silence and the two of us standing together in a room that had known so many years of the three of us, and now held only two.

In the days that followed, as the rituals unfolded and the house slowly returned to something approaching its ordinary rhythm, we went to her cupboard. The sarees were folded and arranged with the care that had characterised everything she did — soft cotton and silk, colours that were hers, familiar in a way that reached below conscious memory into something more cellular. I touched them, and in the touching felt, briefly and vividly, her presence — her standing there, watching with the quiet amusement she brought to moments of sentiment, perhaps smiling at the image of me holding a saree as though it were a relic. Then the feeling passed. Reality, which had been briefly gentle, returned to its actual shape.

I asked Appachi how he would manage. How anyone manages the loss of the person who has been the centre of their daily life for more years than they can count. He considered the question with his characteristic unhurriedness before answering:

> *"We had prepared each other. We both knew, for a long time, that one of us would go first. We spoke about it. We made our peace with it, as much as anyone can. That does not mean it doesn't hurt. It means the hurt was expected. And expected pain is something you can stand in."*

That answer has stayed with me — not as comfort exactly, but as something more durable than comfort. A piece of grown-up wisdom about the relationship between anticipation and grief, between the love that prepares you and the love that breaks you and the understanding that they can be the same love, differently experienced across different stages of time.

He gave me a book then. Lifted it from somewhere in the room and placed it in my hands with the care of someone transferring something that matters. "She asked me to give this to you," he said. The sentence was simple, and it carried the weight of all the things that are left unsaid until the person who would have said them can no longer speak. I held the book and understood that I was holding something beyond its physical object: an intention, a final gesture of the woman who had spent her life giving me things I didn't always know I needed.

The book spoke of trying, of trusting, of moving forward when the path ahead is unclear. It spoke of the particular kind of courage required not for the dramatic moments but for the ordinary ones — the daily recommitment to continuing, the choosing again and again, in the face of every reason to stop, to go on. Its central message was simple: keep trying. In different ways. Through different doors. Until you arrive.

Appachi spoke to me then with a directness that I will always associate with the particular quality of love that tells you true things because it cares too much to tell you comfortable ones:

> *"Create your identity. Find who you are. Find what you are capable of. I am old now. I must learn to stand in new ways. If you stay, you will stay for me — and that would not be good for either of us. Go. Be strong. I am here for you always. But you must move forward. That is what she wanted. That is what I want."*

I could not hear her words again. But I had not lost them. Some people stop speaking, and yet what they have given does not become silent — it continues, in how you live, in what you choose, in who you are determined to become. She had already placed her words inside me, long before she left. All I had to do was listen to the voice she had made in me. It was, I discovered, remarkably like her own.

Chapter – 09 – The man who still woke at four

Some people change when life changes.
And some people simply continue —
not out of denial,
but out of a strength
so deep it has become indistinguishable from character.

The first thing I learned about grief, through watching him, is that it does not always announce itself in the ways we expect. We anticipate collapse. We anticipate the suspension of ordinary behaviour — the inability to eat, to sleep, to maintain the small daily structures that constitute a life. And sometimes this happens. But sometimes grief is carried differently. Sometimes the person who has lost the most continues to wake at four in the morning and walk to the kitchen and make coffee, because that is what they have always done, and the continuing of it is not denial but a different kind of holding on.

Appachi still woke at four. The house was quiet in a new way now — a different quality of quiet from the morning quiet he had always known, which had been the quiet of sleep rather than the quiet of absence. Aatha's kitchen sounds were no longer there. The particular rhythm of her morning — vessel to flame, the small adjustments of a practiced hand, the aroma building gradually from its source — was gone. But he woke into this new quiet and moved through it without collapsing.

He made the coffee himself. The same process, the same sequence of actions, the same result by every measurable standard — the colour, the smell, the heat of it. But not the same feeling. Coffee that has been made by the same hands in the same kitchen for decades carries something beyond its ingredients. It carries the presence of the person who made it. Without that presence, even the most perfect cup tastes of absence. He drank it anyway. Every morning. Because the drinking of it was also a kind of continuity — a refusal to let the love of a thing be erased by the loss of the person who had made the love of it possible.

The household reorganised itself around his solitude with the slow, imperfect effort of any system adapting to a fundamental change. He cooked when he could. On days when the cooking defeated him, he brought food from outside, without apology or self-pity, with the practical equanimity of a man who has made peace with the difference between what was and what now is. The kitchen, which had once moved to Aatha's precise and ordered governance, acquired a gentler dishevelment.

Things were not in quite the places they had been. The system held, but loosely.

Even small things marked the difference. His white vesti — always impeccable in Aatha's time, pressed and arranged with her particular care — was still clean, still worn with dignity, but differently laundered. Not neglected. Just differently attended to. There is a particular tenderness in this kind of detail. It speaks not of a man who has stopped caring for himself but of a man who is learning, at an age when most people have long since established the fixed shapes of their daily lives, to care for himself in new ways.

What did not change was his mind. He read with the same appetite, the same broad interest in everything from current affairs to ancient philosophy. He underlined passages. He folded corners. He shared what he read with his children and grandchildren with the same generosity of a person who has spent a lifetime believing that good ideas should not be kept to themselves. He prepared for retirement with methodical attention — planning the closing of his shop, the orderly transfer of responsibilities, the practical arrangements of a life that was deliberately simplifying itself. There was no drama in this. There was only a man doing what needed doing, one step at a time.

One day he said to me, with a frankness that bypassed sentiment entirely and went directly to the truth:

"I cannot be Aatha. That is not possible and it would be wrong to attempt it. The way she cared — for this house, for all of you — cannot be replicated. It was hers entirely. What I can do is take care of you in the way that is mine. I hope you will be able to receive that, even though it looks different. Even though it is not what you are used to."

And then, before I could speak:

"Be strong. I am here — like a banyan tree. The branches spread. The roots hold. Whatever comes, the tree stands."

I have thought about that image many times since. The banyan tree, which grows its roots downward from its branches, which spreads not by moving away from its centre but by extending itself outward while remaining anchored — it was an apt image for the man who offered it. He was not telling me he was invulnerable, or that he had not been profoundly altered by what he had lost. He was telling me that the alteration had not undone the foundation. The tree stood.

Far away, my own mornings were taking their new shape. I had settled into work — teaching, coaching, the building of something professional and daily that gave the formless hours of a new life a structure to move within. I woke, and I worked, and in the working I carried forward what they had each contributed to who I was — Aatha's patience, her practical intelligence, her instinct for what a person needs; Appachi's discipline, his consistency, his willingness to let difficulty be difficult rather than softening it into something easier to hold.

Coffee still existed in my days, but it was never quite the same. I tried different preparations, different styles, the many variations that the world offers to those who have been made to love the thing. None of them matched. What was missing was not a recipe or a technique. What was missing was irreplaceable: the particular person who had made the morning what it was, who had known without being told how you took it, who had handed it to you as part of an act of love so habituated it had long since ceased to look like love and had simply become the way the day began.

For Appachi, I learned, coffee gradually disappeared. From coffee to tea, and then from tea to milk. A quiet, unremarked migration that said, without words, more than most eulogies manage. We knew what the coffee had meant. We knew what its absence meant. We did not speak about it, because some things are most clearly understood in silence.

> *He had shown me something essential about what it means to continue. Not to be unchanged. Not to be unaffected. But to take the altered shape of your life and keep moving through it, with the same fundamental decency, the same fundamental interest in the people around you, the same fundamental willingness to be of use, that you carried into it. To stand, in other words. To keep standing.*

Chapter – 10 – The mistakes He let me make

Some people teach you by protecting you from mistakes.
He taught me by trusting me enough to make them.

There is a philosophy of education that believes the first responsibility of a teacher is to prevent error — to construct the learning environment so carefully, so precisely, that the student moves through it without stumbling, accumulating knowledge in a clean and orderly way that leaves no room for the messiness and discouragement of getting things wrong. This philosophy is understandable. It is also, I came to believe through the evidence of my own formation, profoundly mistaken.

Appachi operated from a different philosophy entirely, one that he never articulated in theoretical terms because it was simply the natural expression of how he understood people and how they grow. He believed that the experience of making a mistake — a real one, with real consequences, in the actual world rather than a simulated one — was not a failure of teaching but an essential component of it. He believed that knowing and doing are different countries, separated by a distance that cannot be crossed through observation alone. And he acted on this belief with a patient consistency that, at the time, I found variously infuriating, embarrassing, and confusing, and that I now recognise as one of the most significant gifts of my formation.

The bank was a familiar world to me long before I was old enough to conduct business within it. I had been going there since childhood, always accompanied, always in the role of attentive observer. I had sat in the waiting area and watched the movement of people and money and paperwork with the particular absorption that children bring to worlds they do not yet fully understand but are already working to decode. I had asked questions — many questions — and Appachi had answered all of them with his characteristic precision. What is the cashier's role? What makes the money safe? What is the distinction between credit and debit, between a deposit and a withdrawal?

I had absorbed the answers. I had watched the yellow challans filled out, submitted, stamped, returned. I had constructed, from observation alone, a comprehensive mental model of the process. The model was confident. The model was detailed. The model was, as I would shortly discover, crucially incomplete in exactly the way that observation-without-doing always leaves a model incomplete.

The assignment arrived without preamble: take this thousand rupees to the bank and deposit it. A thousand rupees. In my hands. Real money, real task, real bank. I received it with a performance of casual confidence that I did not entirely feel, because this was the kind of assignment one did not want to appear uncertain about. I had seen this done dozens of times. I knew exactly what to do.

The walk to the bank had a different quality than any previous walk there had possessed. Previously, I had walked as a passenger — present but not responsible, observing but not accountable. Now I walked as someone with a purpose, carrying an object of value, about to complete a real transaction in the real world. The distinction was not dramatic but it was felt. Something had shifted in how I held myself.

I entered, found the challans, sat down, and began to fill one out with the careful legibility of someone who wants to do this right. Name. Amount. Date. The pen moved with deliberate confidence across the paper. Before I could finish, an elderly woman appeared at my elbow — thin, quiet, with the tentative manner of someone who has arrived at a place that slightly defeats them. "Papa," she said, "can you write for me also?"

Without a moment's hesitation I said yes. I was, in that moment, the person who knew how this worked. I filled her slip with the same information I was putting on my own, in the same confident hand, and we stood together in the queue — she in front, I behind — waiting for the satisfying conclusion of a task completed.

At the counter, my slip was taken, examined, and then examined again with a quality of attention that was not, I understood with a sinking certainty, the attention of routine verification. A pause. A look. And then: "This is wrong."

The challan was set aside. In one brief exchange at a counter, in front of the elderly woman I had so confidently assisted and the several people behind us in the queue, my comprehensive mental model of the process revealed its crucial gap. Denominations. The way the amount was to be written — not simply as a number but in the specific, structured form the document required. The detail I had never noticed in all my hours of observation because I had never been the one filling the form.

I walked home with a quality of feeling that I can describe only as the specific compound of anger and shame and humiliation that comes from being revealed as less competent than you presented yourself to be. The anger was partially at the situation, partially at myself for my overconfidence, and partially — I will admit this honestly — at the people who had sent me. I had been sent to do something I was not fully equipped to do. That felt, in the immediate heat of it, like a betrayal.

I entered the house with no ceremony, no courtesy, no removal of my footwear at the door as was proper. I spoke the full volume of my frustration without waiting for a suitable moment:

> *"How could you send me like that? Without telling me everything I needed to know? I stood there looking like I had no idea what I was doing — and I didn't! I helped someone else and then we were both wrong together. That is not acceptable."*

It was not a dignified response. It was the response of a child who has been embarrassed and has not yet developed sufficient self-possession to absorb the embarrassment without externalising it. Aatha gave me water without comment. "Drink. Relax." Appachi listened to all of it without interrupting, without the defensiveness of someone who is being accused, with the undefended openness of a man who had expected exactly this and was prepared to receive it.

When the room had quieted, he asked the question that he had evidently been holding in reserve:

"When I gave you this task, did you take the time to understand it fully before you began?"

I said yes. Inside, I knew the truth. He smiled at the inside truth, the smile of a person who sees clearly and holds what he sees without wielding it.

"I knew that writing numbers was not the challenge for you. That was never the point of giving you this amount. I wanted you to encounter denomination. The real structure of the process. You cannot learn that from watching. You can only learn it from doing — and sometimes from doing it wrong first."

Then, after a pause that carried its own weight:

"Nothing happened. Now you know. Once you know a thing properly — really know it, from the inside, from having gotten it wrong and then gotten it right — you won't repeat the mistake. Failure is not bad. It is the

material from which correction is made. But the comeback must be stronger than the fall."

He paused again, and added something I have carried since then into every classroom and coaching session I have ever conducted:

"If something is not corrected at five, it will not change at fifty."

Ten days later, he handed me three thousand rupees and asked me to deposit it. I did not rush. I went home first and practiced on paper. I looked up the form. I worked through the denomination structure with deliberate, unhurried attention. I arrived at the bank with the specific confidence of someone who has prepared rather than assumed, who knows the difference.

The slip was completed correctly. It was verified, stamped, returned with a brief "Good" from the staff member, who had no idea that those two syllables were landing on someone who had been waiting ten days to hear them.

He didn't protect me from failure. He introduced me to it with full intention, because he understood that the version of me who had been through it — who had felt the embarrassment and sat with it and prepared and gone back — would be permanently more capable than the version who had only ever watched from a safe distance. That is not cruelty. That is a very specific and very deep form of love.

Chapter – 11 – Evenings on the platform

He did not sit me down and teach me about life.
He took me to the railway station
and let life do it.

Childhood in the nineteen-nineties had a particular texture that is difficult to convey to those who did not live inside it. The days were longer, or seemed longer — not because time actually passed more slowly, but because time was not yet divided into the frantic, screen-mediated increments that would come later. There were hours in the afternoon that belonged to no particular purpose. There were evenings that unfolded at their own pace without the urgency of notifications and updates and the constant low-grade sense that elsewhere, something more interesting was happening.

Many of my best evenings, in those years, were with Appachi. Not doing anything remarkable. Not going anywhere expensive or memorable in the conventional sense. Simply going — to a park, to a temple, through the neighbourhood on a walk that had no fixed destination. He was an unhurried man in all things, and his unhurriedness was contagious. In his company, I moved more slowly. I noticed more. I had not yet learned to call this anything; I simply knew that evenings with Appachi had a quality that other evenings lacked.

I had received, at some point, a toy train. Not a sophisticated one — just the kind of simple, pleasing object that a child can run through its imaginary landscape for hours without diminishing interest. I was not the kind of child who destroyed toys out of curiosity or excess energy. I played carefully, with the particular seriousness that children bring to the things they genuinely love, and then I put the train away in its place, and the next day I took it out again. The train stayed.

One afternoon, cycling through channels on the television, I found a programme about trains. Engines and carriages, tracks and signals, the whole working world of rail rendered on screen with an immediacy that connected, without warning, to the object in my hand. What I had been imagining in miniature was suddenly real and large and moving. I did not say much about it aloud. But Appachi noticed — he had a quality of attention to the people around him that missed very little — and he acted on what he noticed in the way he always acted on observations: quietly, without announcement, as though what he was doing were simply the obvious natural response to an obvious natural fact.

He began taking me to the railway station. Not once. Not as a special occasion or a treat. Regularly, as one of the ordinary rhythms of our shared evenings together.

The railway station was not, I came to understand through those visits, merely a functional place where journeys began and ended. It was a complete world — compressed, heterogeneous, alive with every register of human experience occurring simultaneously. The air itself was different there: diesel and metal, the particular dusty warmth of platforms, the smell of food from the canteen mixing with the smell of motion and distance. Vendors moved through the crowds with sundal and peanuts and water and small fried things that tasted exactly like themselves — not like home cooking, not like restaurant food, but like railway platform food, which is its own flavour and belongs to no other context.

The trains arrived with their own physics of approach. You heard them before you saw them — a low vibration at the periphery of perception that built steadily, that became felt through the soles of your feet before it became heard through your ears. Then the shape emerging at the far end of the platform, growing with a speed that always seemed too fast for something so large and then, suddenly, the train was there, filling your entire field of vision, the sheer metal presence of it, the noise, the displacement of air. And then it passed. And then the silence — which was not actually silence, because the platform sounds continued, but felt like silence after the roar, felt like the world catching its breath.

I told Appachi once that this was my favourite part. The silence after. He considered this, and then said:

> *"All big difficulties are like that. At first, they feel overwhelming — heavy, loud, too large to look at directly. But if you stay in them, if you don't run from the noise and the weight, what comes on the other side is peace. The silence is the reward for having stayed."*

He said it simply, the way he said most things. He was not lecturing. He was not being pedagogical. He was sharing, as one shares an observation with a person in whose company one is comfortable, something that the moment had suggested. The simplicity of the delivery was part of its power. If he had said it with the gravity of a lesson, I might have resisted it. Said this way — offhandedly, as a natural extension of what we were already talking about — it went in without resistance and stayed.

One evening, we saw a group of boys at the far end of the platform. They were throwing stones at a passing train, aiming for the undercarriage, some metallurgical curiosity drawing them to the magnets and mechanisms that live beneath a moving train. I was disturbed by this in the way that children are disturbed by rule-breaking — not with the adult's understanding of specific danger but with the simpler alarm of knowing that something is wrong.

"Why are they doing that?" I asked.

"They want the magnets from the wheels," he said. "They don't know the consequence. They're not bad people — they're simply people who haven't yet been shown the danger."

"But it's wrong," I said. "We should stop them."

He looked at them for a moment with his characteristic calm, and then looked at me:

"They are not ready to hear it yet. If we go to them now and tell them to stop, they will stop in front of us and resume when we leave. The intervention has to

happen in the right way, with the right people, at the right moment. Otherwise it doesn't take. We move."

I was not satisfied with this. The injustice of non-intervention sat uncomfortably with me, and I said so. He did not argue. We moved.

Two days later, we returned to the same platform, the same bench. The boys were there again. But so were railway officials, and the boys were standing before them with a different posture — not throwing, but listening. Someone was speaking to them about danger, about what happens to a human body near a moving train, about the life that can be lost in a second of bad judgment. The boys were listening with the specific attention of people who are genuinely receiving something rather than merely enduring an authority figure's words.

I looked at Appachi. He said nothing. He did not need to. The action had already been taken — not in front of me, not as a demonstration, but in the right way with the right people at the right time, exactly as he had said. He had not decided to do nothing. He had decided to do the thing that would actually work.

I have never forgotten that evening. The lesson in it was not simple — it was about the difference between the impulse toward justice and the wisdom of how to pursue it effectively, between reacting from feeling and acting from understanding. He taught me that the quality of an intervention matters as much as its intention. That timing is not passive. It is its own form of action.

Those evenings on the platform were not about trains, though I loved the trains. They were a curriculum delivered so quietly, in such unprepossessing settings, that I absorbed it without ever knowing I was being taught. That was his genius as a teacher — the complete absence of the pedagogical manner that makes children aware they are receiving a lesson and therefore brace themselves against it. He simply brought me alongside him and let me watch him think, and in watching him think, I learned how to think.

Chapter – 12 – The strength He built without speaking

He didn't remove the obstacles from my path.
He prepared me to walk through them.
He didn't protect me from pain.
He gave me the strength to face it.

He never called me by my name alone. In all the years I spent in his company, through childhood and adolescence and the early adult years when I was still close enough to that house to be shaped by its daily presence, he called me "Aatha." Not in the context of the Tamil word's familial meaning, but as a name he had chosen for me — a personal designation that said something about how he saw me, about the respect he intended by the address, about the kind of person he was speaking to each time he spoke.

I was old enough, by the time I thought about this, to understand how rare it was. Most men of his generation — of any generation — did not lead with this kind of conscious, deliberate regard for the dignity of the women and girls around them. It was not always absent, but it was often unstated, implicit, assumed rather than expressed. He expressed it. Not once, not in a moment of particular tenderness, but as the baseline of how he engaged — with his wife, with his daughters, with me, with every woman he encountered. The tone was different. Always measured, always aware, always carrying in its very quality the message: you are someone to be addressed with care.

I watched him with Aatha over years of their marriage — years that had long since passed the stage where newness does the work of holding two people together, when what keeps a relationship alive is nothing more or less than the daily choice to honour the person you have chosen. He never spoke to her with the casual disrespect that creeps into long partnerships — the shorthand that shades into dismissal, the impatience that becomes the ambient temperature of a shared life. When they disagreed, the disagreement stayed contained, never escalating beyond what the moment required. A pause. A look. The private negotiation of two people who have developed, over decades, the vocabulary for settling their differences without making a battlefield of the space between them. Then the conversation continued.

He also took me places. Not to significant destinations but to ordinary ones — parks, temples, exhibitions, neighbourhood spots that held no particular landmark value but acquired it through his presence and attention.

We went by cycle when the distance was short, with me sitting behind him, the city passing at the pace of someone who intends to see it rather than simply transit through it. Those rides had a particular quality — the physical closeness, the motion, the unhurried pace of observation — that made them one of the most reliable sites of real conversation. Something about movement loosens the tongue.

One evening, returning from a park as the sky shifted into its evening register — the quality of light changing, the first lamps beginning to appear in shop windows, the particular urban twilight that transforms a familiar street into something briefly unfamiliar — I saw a wedding hall. It was impossible not to see. It was lit with the extravagance that such occasions require, decorated with colours that competed with each other for supremacy, populated by people in their most elaborate and joyful clothing, the whole thing pulsing with the collective energy of a hundred people committed to a single day's celebration.

I reacted to it with the full unreserved enthusiasm of someone who has not yet developed the capacity to modulate their public responses. I spoke loudly. I pointed. I turned on the cycle seat to look, which is precisely the action that one should not take while another person is balancing a bicycle and navigating a street. The physics of the situation resolved itself immediately: the bicycle went one way, we went another, the ground arrived.

Pain came sharp and comprehensive — a scraped leg, burning palms, the dull impact of a fall that had been too fast to brace against. I lay on the pavement for a moment and then sat up and waited for the response that the situation, by every convention I had observed, clearly warranted: urgency, concern, the particular anxious overreaction of an adult whose charge has been injured.

What I received was different. He looked at me from the pavement, entirely composed, and asked simply: "Are you okay?"

I communicated the presence of pain. He acknowledged it:

"Yes. Pain will be there."

And then, with perfect equanimity:

"Be calm. Ten minutes and we are home. Aatha will look after it. It is a small thing. Come. Let us go."

The composure in this confused me more than the fall itself. I had been hurt. I had been on the ground. I had expected the full theatrical apparatus of adult concern, and what I had received instead was acknowledgement and direction and an implicit expectation that I was capable of handling both. We reached home. The injury was attended to with Aatha's characteristic competent efficiency. And then I sat with the question of what had happened — not the fall, but the response to it.

After some time, I put the question directly:

"Why are you like this? Other people react when someone they care about is hurt. You don't. There was no fear in you. No urgency. It felt like you didn't care."

He listened to all of this, and then said, with the gentleness of someone who is about to say something that will sound harder than it is:

"It was a small wound. And I thought you were stronger than this. I believed, from watching you, that you would accept the pain and move forward. Was I wrong?"

The morning after, everyone in the house anticipated that I would remain home, recovering, sparing myself the discomfort of a school day with an injured leg. Instead, I woke and wrote a letter formally requesting permission to attend in a half-uniform, as wearing shoes was not yet possible. And I went to school — not in defiance of the injury but in conversation with it, carrying it alongside the rest of what I carried, moving forward because forward was the direction I had been shown.

He had not manufactured this response in me through instruction. He had built it, over years of consistent exposure to a particular way of being in the world — a way that held difficulty without being undone by it, that acknowledged pain without dramatising it, that moved through hardship with the quiet efficiency of someone who has simply decided that hardship will not be the thing that stops them.

There was also the matter of the words I had brought home from the playground. Children acquire language in the way they acquire everything — through imitation of what surrounds them, without necessarily understanding the full weight of what they are taking on. I had picked up words that had a certain swagger to them, words that made me feel, in the narrow social economy of children playing outside, like someone who knew things. I used them with the confidence of the uninitiated.

He said nothing immediately. He waited until the right moment — until the household had quieted, until the evening had reached the hour when conversations of this kind could be received rather than deflected. Then:

> *"Respect should come from calmness. From affection. Not from fear, not from the kind of force that makes people pretend to respect you while waiting for you to look away. The second kind is not respect at all. It is compliance. A smile should be your signature — the thing people remember when they think of you. That is what a leader carries. Not noise. Not sharpness. Warmth. And the strength that warmth, when it is genuine, actually contains."*

He corrected with timing rather than with anger. He waited until the person in front of him was in a state to receive what was being offered, because he understood that correction aimed at a closed mind produces nothing but defensiveness. He shaped the container before he poured anything into it. That is, I came to understand, the highest level of the teaching instinct — not the transmission of content but the preparation of the person to receive it.

Chapter – 13 – The journeys that stayed

Travel is not about distance.
It is about who walks beside you.
The same place, at a different age,
with a different person,
becomes an entirely different world.

There is a category of journey that ends when you arrive home. The luggage is unpacked, the photographs are sorted, the experience is filed away in the completed section of memory, and life resumes its ordinary shape. These are not bad journeys. They are perfectly adequate journeys. They have their pleasures and their stories. But they do not leave a permanent residue. They do not change the person who takes them.

And then there is the other kind.

At the time I decided to travel with Aatha, I was travelling often for chess tournaments — the particular nomadism of competitive sport, moving through cities and hotels and tournament halls, always with teammates, always embedded in the social ecosystem of a group of people who shared a purpose. Those journeys had their own rhythm, their own pleasures. Cards played in train compartments. Food shared across laps. The comfortable noise of a group of people who know each other well. I was not unhappy in them.

But something was missing. Not excitement — there was excitement. Not companionship — there was companionship. What was missing, I think, was depth. The depth that comes from being with someone who knows you in the way that precedes everything else, who knew you before you knew yourself, who carries in their presence a reference to your entire history. I wanted a journey that was more than movement. I wanted one that meant something.

The decision to take Aatha felt, from the moment I made it, like the beginning of something. We boarded the train for a long journey — thirty-six hours — and settled into our compartment with the slightly self-conscious awareness of two people who are, for the first time, in a travelling context without the usual scaffolding of family around them. Just the two of us. Just the train. Just everything ahead.

The compartment filled with the random assemblage of people that long-distance rail travel produces — strangers from different cities and different lives, thrown together by the commonality of a destination, arranged in the specific proximity of shared berths and the indefinite intimacy of a day and a half in the same enclosed space. Initially, as always in such situations, the social contract of non-interaction held. Everyone maintained their private sphere. Bags were barriers. Books were signals. Everyone was politely, efficiently alone.

This lasted a few hours. Then, as it always does on long journeys when people are not in too much of a hurry to be anywhere, the membrane of sociability began to soften. Food was opened — and with food, an offer: does anyone want some? Snacks were accepted across the aisle. Someone produced cards. Laughter arrived, as laughter does, without having been invited, without ceremony, as the natural result of several people in a small space having decided that enjoyment was more interesting than withdrawal. The compartment became, by the end of the evening, a small world unto itself — a temporary community assembled by accident and held together by the simple shared experience of moving through the same dark country at the same speed toward the same distant point.

I woke late the next morning, somewhere in the middle of that duration of travel that is neither departure nor arrival, to find Aatha not in her berth but sitting with the other passengers as though she had known them for a decade. She was talking, genuinely engaged, listening with the full quality of her attention, laughing with the ease of someone who is exactly where they belong. She had bought sweets from a passing vendor and was distributing them with the generosity that she brought to everything, not calculating, not measuring, simply giving because giving was what the moment called for.

I watched her for several long minutes before she noticed me, and what I felt watching her was something between confusion and awe.

"You know these people?" I asked, when she finally turned and saw me.

She looked at me with the expression of someone who is about to say something simple and important:

"No."

One word. But it dismantled something in my understanding. I had been watching what I thought was the relaxed behaviour of old friends, and it was not that at all. It was the relaxed behaviour of someone who had decided that the absence of prior acquaintance was not a reason to be closed. Who had looked at a group of strangers and chosen, without hesitation, without the social anxiety that makes most of us hold back until we feel sufficiently certain of a welcome, to connect. Not to introduce herself in the formal way of a person seeking acceptance, but simply to be present with people — fully, warmly, with her whole self — and let the connection form from that.

It was, I realised, exactly what she did everywhere. The same quality of presence she brought to the people of the neighbourhood, to the friends who came to her with their troubles, to the strangers who asked her directions. She did not grade people by their relationship to her before deciding how much of herself to offer. She simply offered. The grade she applied was not social — it was intuitive. She could read what a person needed and give it, without requiring prior knowledge of them, because her attention to the human being in front of her was sufficient to tell her what was required.

I began, on that journey, to learn the language she was speaking. Imperfectly, with the self-consciousness of a student who is aware of their own efforts, but genuinely. I spoke to people. I offered food. I asked questions and actually listened to the answers. The journey became, in this way, more than thirty-six hours of transit. It became a master class in the particular skill of being present with strangers — which is to say, of treating the accidental companion with the same care you bring to the people you have chosen.

That journey also contained a lesson of a different kind. The physical toll of the long travel — dehydration, fatigue, the accumulated strain of sleeping and waking in a moving carriage — arrived not immediately upon landing but shortly after, when the excitement of arrival had faded and the body was finally permitted to make its situation known. Before I had fully registered the extent of what I was feeling, Aatha had already assessed it. She called Appachi. Contacts were activated, relatives were reached, transport was arranged. Within two hours, the situation had been resolved, and I was comfortable and attended to.

She did not panic, and this was the thing I noticed most. No raised voice. No dramatic declaration of the severity of the situation. Simply a rapid, clear-eyed assessment of what was needed, followed by the most direct available path to getting it. The calmness was not indifference — I felt entirely cared for. It was competence. The calmness of someone who knows that panic is never the most efficient response to a crisis, and who has practised, over a lifetime, the art of responding to difficulty with the minimum of emotional overhead.

Once I was settled, she guided me through the remaining days of the trip with a slightly different quality of attention than before — not protective exactly, but watchful, making sure that independence was being rebuilt at the right pace, that I was not being allowed to remain passive simply because the earlier problem had given passivity an excuse. She was not interested in keeping me dependent on her management. She was interested in returning me to my own competence, enriched.

> *Years later, I stood in that same place alone. The geography was identical. The streets were the same streets. But the journey was different, because I was different — and because the differences had been built, in no small part, by her. Memory walked with me in her absence, pointing to things she would have noticed, asking questions she would have asked. That is how the people who love us travel with us even when they are not there. They have already become part of how we see.*

Chapter – 14 – Together but not connected

We are moving together.
We are eating together.
We are sitting at the same table.
And yet — somehow —
we are not in the same place at all.

We are busier today than any generation before us. This is the fact we repeat to ourselves constantly, almost proudly, as though the quantity of our busyness is evidence of something important — of a life fully lived, of a purpose seriously pursued. We have more tools, more devices, more platforms, more ways of reaching one another across distance than our parents could have imagined and our grandparents would not have believed. We are connected, the technology tells us, to everything and everyone.

And yet.

Aatha and Appachi had none of this. No smartphone in the pocket. No notification arriving every few minutes with the urgent news that someone, somewhere, had posted something that required acknowledgement. What they had instead was something that we have quietly, without quite deciding to, traded away: the unbroken attention of the person sitting beside them. The support system of genuine presence. The particular richness of a life in which, when you were with someone, you were entirely with them.

The difference is not about technology at all. It is about what we have allowed technology to replace. Their generation had no devices — but they had each other, completely and unhurriedly, without the divided attention that has become the baseline of modern intimacy. They had neighbours who came and stayed. Children who sat with grandparents and heard their stories. Marriages conducted at the speed of conversation, not the speed of a scroll. The support systems they built were made of people, and people require time, and they gave the time without experiencing it as sacrifice.

We are running, most of us, without a clear answer to the question of what we are running toward. Ask a person why they are in such a hurry and they will tell you they have things to do. Ask them what things. They will mention work, responsibilities, commitments. Ask them whether those commitments bring them closer to what they actually value. The question will land strangely, because most of us have stopped asking it of ourselves.

We go shopping not because we need anything but because there is a sale, and the sale creates the feeling of opportunity, and opportunity has been trained in us to feel like something that must not be missed. We buy the thing. We bring it home. We feel, briefly, the pleasant hum of acquisition. And then we are running again — toward the next thing, the next offer, the next update, without ever quite arriving anywhere.

We move out because everyone is moving out. We post updates because everyone is posting updates. We curate the appearance of a full life and offer it to the world as evidence. But the question that goes unasked — the question Aatha and Appachi would have asked without hesitation — is this: was the evening actually felt? Were the people in the photograph actually present to each other? Or were they simply present in the same location, which is an entirely different thing?

Think about what a family outing is supposed to be. The original intention behind it is simple: to feel refreshed. To be with each other in a way that the routine doesn't permit. To talk, to notice things together, to return home carrying something more than you left with.

And then think about what it has largely become.

The family arrives at the restaurant. The menu is opened and photographed. The order is placed. And then the waiting begins — ten or fifteen minutes that are, in theory, the gift of unstructured time, the small opening in which conversation could happen, in which someone might say something true or funny or quietly important. In practice, the phones emerge. The children have their screens. The adults have theirs. The table holds seven people and seven separate interior worlds, none of them touching.

Then something happens. The table beside yours receives their food first. They arrived after you. This is the moment that produces the evening's only real emotion — not warmth, not the pleasure of being with people you love, but indignation. How could they get their food before us? The waiter is summoned. The grievance is presented with the gravity of a genuine injustice. The food arrives. It is eaten without comment — good or bad, worth returning for or not, all of it absorbed in silence. The bill is paid. Everyone moves toward the exit.

The family has moved together. Physically, they have spent two hours in proximity. And yet they have not connected. Not once, across the entire evening, did anything happen between them that could not have happened with strangers. The table held the warmth of bodies but not the warmth of people who are genuinely with each other.

I write this not with judgment but with recognition. I have sat at that table too. I have been the person checking the phone while someone I love was trying to catch my eye. I have let the small, ordinary beauty of an evening slip past while I was occupied with something less important. We all have. The habit is so pervasive that we have stopped noticing it as a habit and begun to accept it as simply the way things are.

> *You are running for your family. But they have to feel your effort. They have to feel your presence. No device, however advanced, can explain to the people who love you how much they mean to you. Only you can do that. Only your attention — sustained, unhurried, fully given — can do that.*

Run long. But run with clarity. Know what you are running toward. And pause, sometimes, long enough to find out whether the people running beside you can actually feel you there.

Chapter – 15 – The table that held everything

Some tables are just surfaces.
And some tables become the place
where you first understood
what it means to be truly with someone.

I remember a day trip. Not to anywhere famous or expensive — simply to a place worth going, where the going itself was the point. Aatha and Appachi had been awake before the sun, before the street, before the city had decided it was morning. They had packed everything the night before with the quiet efficiency of people who understand that preparation is itself a form of care: idli, soft and warm, wrapped in the particular way that keeps them that way through a journey. Dried banana leaf parcels, three of them, one for each of us — breakfast for the arrival and dinner for the return. Everything thought about. Everything ready.

We travelled in the early light, when the roads still belonged to the few rather than the many. I remember the particular quality of that morning — the coolness still in the air, the sense of being ahead of the day rather than behind it, the mild excitement of going somewhere before the rest of the world had finished waking. When we arrived, we walked. Real walking — the kind that asks something of you, that builds warmth slowly in the muscles, that makes the ground feel real beneath your feet. The day grew warmer as it passed. We moved through it together, sweating, occasionally tired, occasionally stopping, but always moving.

By the time we reached the hotel for a rest, I had earned my exhaustion completely. We used the washroom. We found a table. And then the air conditioning reached us.

There is a specific pleasure that belongs only to this moment: the cold air of an air-conditioned room landing on a body that has been warm for hours, touching damp skin, arriving without announcement. It is one of those small physical experiences that require no enhancement and permit no improvement. I sat down and bent my head onto the table — not in unhappiness but in the comfortable, satisfied heaviness of someone who has done something real with their body and is now resting it.

From that position — head resting on my arms, eyes not quite closed, the cool air moving slowly around me — I heard them begin to talk.

Near our table, on the wall or on a display somewhere in the room, there was a piece of Warli art. Aatha noticed it in the way she noticed everything — with her full attention, with genuine curiosity, as though whatever she was looking at deserved the complete effort of her interest. She began to speak about it, softly, more to Appachi than to me, though I heard every word.

She spoke about the colour — the stark white figures on the dark ground, the way the contrast created its own kind of depth. She spoke about the forms: the human figures arranged not as individuals but as community, each one part of a larger movement, a larger purpose. Unity is strength, she said. Look at how they are always in groups, always doing something together — dancing, farming, celebrating. No single figure is the centre. The community is the centre. That, she said quietly, is the message. Not painted on top of the art. Painted into it.

Appachi leaned forward. He looked where she was pointing and found something she had not mentioned, or had not yet reached: the geometric forms, the triangles and circles that structured the composition. He said — with the particular delight of a man who has noticed something that genuinely pleases him — that the hotel was using its walls to teach. Farming, he said. These shapes represent the cycle of cultivation, the relationship between people and land, the knowledge that has been carried forward through generations in a language that requires no literacy, only looking. The art, he said, is a record. It is memory given a form that can be passed on.

They talked about the lamps depicted in the artwork — the old styles, the particular shapes that belonged to households of an earlier time. They spoke about what those lamps meant: not merely the absence of darkness but the presence of something warmer, more intentional. A lamp in a home was once an act of care. It was placed, tended, protected from wind. Its light was not assumed. It was made, each evening, by someone who understood that warmth must be created and maintained, that it does not arrive on its own.

The food came at some point during this conversation. They made sure I had enough, asked if I wanted anything more, and then returned to their talking. I lifted my head at some stage and looked at what they had been describing — the Warli figures on the wall, the geometric patterns, the lamps — and saw it all with their eyes before I had developed my own. That is the gift of being young in the company of people who pay attention: you inherit their way of seeing before you have formed your own, and it stays with you, a foundation you did not build but will stand on for the rest of your life.

In the years since, I have been to many more hotels. I have sat at tables with more impressive décor, more elaborate menus, more attentive service. I have been to places designed with professional precision to produce exactly the feeling of ease and pleasure that a good outing is supposed to generate. And I cannot tell you, with any confidence, what happened at most of those tables. I cannot tell you what was discussed or noticed or shared. The evenings passed pleasantly enough. They left almost nothing behind.

But I can tell you exactly what happened at that table after the day trip. I can tell you what Aatha said about unity in the Warli figures and what Appachi saw in the geometric forms. I can tell you about the lamps and what they represented and the particular satisfaction on his face when he explained it. I can tell you the temperature of the air conditioning and the weight of my own tiredness and the quality of light in that room and the sound of their voices talking about something beautiful while I rested and listened and absorbed.

I can tell you because I was actually there. Not performing the experience for anyone else. Not managing a divided attention between the present moment and some parallel existence on a screen. Simply and completely present at that table, in that room, with those two people — head down, ears open, quietly receiving everything they were giving without knowing they were giving it.

That is the difference between a table that holds everything and a table that holds nothing. It is not the food. It is not the setting. It is not the quality of the service or the beauty of the room. It is the quality of attention brought to the table by the people sitting at it. Their willingness to look at what is on the walls, to speak about what they see, to be curious together, to let the evening go wherever genuine conversation takes it rather than managing it toward a conclusion.

Aatha and Appachi did not plan to teach me anything on that trip. They were not constructing a lesson. They were simply being themselves — two people who paid attention to the world, who found things worth talking about everywhere they looked, who were genuinely interested in each other's thoughts about a piece of art on a hotel wall in the middle of an ordinary afternoon.

> *And because they were fully present, I remember it completely. Because they were paying attention, I learned how to pay attention. Because they were with each other and with me — entirely, without reservation — I understood, without anyone having to explain it, what it feels like to be truly at a table with someone.*

That understanding has never left me. I carry it into every room I enter, every meal I sit down to, every moment when I feel the pull of distraction and choose, instead, to look up and be where I actually am.

Some tables are just surfaces. That one held everything.

Chapter – 16 – The smile I wore outside

Pain does not always announce itself.
Sometimes it simply settles in quietly
and waits —
while you smile at the world
and carry on.

There is a particular kind of alone that does not come from being without people. It comes from being without the right people — the ones who know you deeply enough that you do not have to explain yourself before you can be understood. That was the alone I came back to after everything was done. Settled abroad again. Life resuming its outward shape. But inside, something was completely different.

Within those first sixty days, two things happened that I had no preparation for. My body went through a loss — quiet, private, physically and emotionally exhausting in ways that do not have clean language. And Aatha was gone. The one person I would have gone to with exactly this. The one channel that had never required me to compose myself before speaking. Both at once. The body hollowed out and the heart's safest place closed, in the same short season.

I felt like someone blindfolded in a dense forest. Not lost in a dramatic way — just unable to see clearly in any direction, unable to find the edge of the trees, moving carefully and slowly and hoping the ground ahead was solid.

What kept me upright, in those months, was watching Appachi from a distance.

Every time we spoke on the phone, he was clear. Present. He asked about my life with genuine interest and listened to the answers without making the conversation about his own pain. And I knew his pain was enormous — decades of shared mornings, shared conversations, the whole architecture of a daily life built around one person, now gone. He was carrying all of that. But he carried it somewhere the phone call could not reach. When he was with you, he was with you completely.

I watched this and understood it not as the absence of grief but as a decision made inside it. He had found a place for the pain — a corner of himself where it could live without taking over the whole house. He was not performing strength. He was practising it, quietly, every single day.

I decided I would try to do the same. Not because it was easy. Because it was the only direction that led somewhere worth going.

But suppressing pain without releasing it somewhere is not strength. It is pressure. And pressure, held long enough without an outlet, finds its own exit.

Mine came in the middle of the night. I would wake in the small hours — two, sometimes three in the morning — and the silence of the apartment would feel too full. I reached for paper. And I wrote.

Not carefully. Not for anyone to read. With the unguarded honesty of someone speaking to the one person they have always trusted completely. They were letters to Aatha. I wrote to her the way I had always spoken to her — without editing, without the careful arrangement of words that shapes what we say to most people. Everything that had no other place to go went onto those pages. The loss. The loneliness. The things I was afraid of. The conversations I had been composing in my head with no one to receive them.

She had been my channel. The place where nothing needed explaining and nothing would be judged. When that place closed, I had to make one for myself. The paper became it.

When I finished writing, something in me released. Not everything. Not permanently. But enough. Then I would fold the pages and tear them — carefully, completely, into the smallest pieces I could manage. Not in anger. In completion. The words had done their work. I threw them away and went back to sleep.

I did this for months. And slowly, across those months, the weight shifted. The pain did not disappear. But I learned where to put it. I learned how to carry it without wearing it on my face.

The smile I wore outside was not a performance. It was a practice. The daily choice to be present to the people around me even while something inside was still being rebuilt. To not let what I was carrying become the only thing I offered to the world.

> *It was, I realised, exactly what both of them had always done. Appachi at four in the morning making his coffee. Aatha receiving everyone else's troubles while quietly managing her own. They had never taught me this directly. But they had lived it in front of*

me for years. And when the moment came that I needed it most, it was already there — waiting inside me, ready, because they had put it there long before I knew I would need it.

She was no longer there to receive me. So I had to learn to receive myself. To hold my own truth with something approaching the gentleness she had always brought to everything she held.

That was the hardest thing she ever gave me. And she gave it, as she gave everything, not by explaining it — but by leaving me in the one situation where I had no choice but to find it for myself.

Chapter – 17 – The voice that travelled with me

You cannot pack a person into a suitcase.
But you can carry them —
in the way you make a decision,
in the way you hold your nerve,
in the steady voice that speaks
when everything around you is unfamiliar.

There comes a point in the life of two people building something together abroad when the question of where to go next is no longer only about opportunity or logistics. It is about identity. About what each person needs in order to remain themselves while also remaining together. When the time came for a transfer — the ordinary rhythm of a working life that moves from city to city, country to country — the expected thing would have been to pack up and follow. To keep the unit intact by keeping it together in the same place.

I decided not to do the expected thing.

Not because the relationship was uncertain. Not because the future was unclear. But because something in me understood, with a quiet but firm conviction, that this move required me to stand in my own ground for a moment before planting myself in new soil. I was not going back to my native place. I was not moving with my partner immediately. I was, for a defined and deliberate period, choosing to be exactly where I was — to finish what I had started, to close what needed closing, with a full heart rather than a hurried one.

We spent the last days in our shared space the way people spend the last days of something they have genuinely loved — with a particular quality of attention, noticing things they had stopped noticing in the comfort of routine. The apartment that had been ordinary became, in those final days, something worth looking at carefully. The light in the mornings. The way the kitchen smelled after cooking. The specific comfort of a life arranged to your own preferences, in a space that had absorbed the texture of your daily existence. Premium, yes — but the premium was not in the furnishings. It was in what had been built there between two people over time.

The goodbyes, when they came, were temporary. We both knew this. But temporary goodbyes still require a strong heart — perhaps more than permanent ones, because they ask you to feel the weight of the separation while simultaneously trusting the future enough to walk into it alone.

He moved first. And then it was my turn.

I wound everything down. Not quickly, not carelessly — but with the methodical attention of someone who understands that endings deserve the same care as beginnings. The friendships built over those years, the mentors who had given their time and their trust, the professional connections that had grown from tentative introductions into something real and mutual — I packed all of it with me. Not in a suitcase. In the specific, irreplaceable form in which relationships are carried: in memory, in gratitude, in the intention to honour what had been given by becoming someone worthy of it.

The key was the last thing.

There is something about handing over a key that is unlike any other act of closure. It is so small — a piece of metal, a few grams, fitting in the palm of your hand — and yet it carries the full weight of everything that happened behind the door it once opened. I held it for a moment before I gave it up. Not in hesitation. In acknowledgement. This place had held something important. I was leaving it intact, and leaving it grateful, and leaving with more than I had arrived with.

Then I gave it over and walked out with a strong heart and a clear vision of what was ahead. Not certainty — certainty was never the thing Aatha and Appachi had given me. What they had given me was better: the confidence that I could handle what I could not yet see.

The new country received me the way new places always do — with complete indifference. No one was waiting. No one knew my name or my history or the specific combination of things I had just been through. I was a new person in a new place, and the place had no opinion about me whatsoever, which is both the most disorienting and the most freeing feeling a person can have.

There was no support in the conventional sense. No familiar face at the end of the day. No one to call when something went wrong who could arrive within the hour. Everything — the practical arrangements, the social navigation, the daily work of building a liveable life from scratch in an unfamiliar context — was mine to do alone.

And I did it.

Not without difficulty. Not without the particular exhaustion that comes from having to be competent at everything simultaneously, with no one to hand even the smallest task to. But I did it. And what I found, in the doing of it, was that I was not as alone as the external circumstances suggested. Because inside me, the voices were there. Aatha's calm certainty when a situation required problem-solving. Appachi's unhurried steadiness when the pressure mounted. The specific quality of their patience — not passive, but active, a patience that kept working even while it waited.

They had not travelled with me in any physical sense. But they were present in every decision I made, in the way I approached strangers, in the way I held difficulty without catastrophising it, in the way I kept my eyes on what needed doing rather than on everything that could go wrong. I had absorbed them so thoroughly, over so many years of watching and listening, that they had become part of how I thought. They were not memories I consulted. They were instincts I trusted.

That is the deepest form of inheritance. Not what you remember about a person, but what you have become because of them — so woven into your own nature that you can no longer separate where they end and you begin.

Slowly, the new place began to yield. The contacts came — people in my field, people who spoke the same professional language, people who recognised the work and received it with genuine interest. The network that had taken years to build in the previous place began, in compressed and accelerated form, to rebuild itself here. It did not happen overnight. But it happened, because I made it happen, with the same quiet consistency that I had watched two people practice across an entire lifetime.

And then, after more than a month of standing alone in that new ground and finding that it held my weight, something shifted in my thinking. The distance from my partner had served its purpose. I had proven, to myself and to no one else, that I could do this alone. That the strength was mine, not borrowed, not dependent on proximity to someone else's certainty.

Having proven it, I no longer needed to keep proving it.

I moved to where he was. Not because I had to. Because I chose to — from a position of fullness rather than need, from the clear-eyed recognition that partnership is not a weakness but a foundation, and that a foundation is only valuable if you are willing to stand on it. We laid the base there together. The months that followed were not easy — new place, new systems, new challenges arriving before the previous ones had been fully resolved. But each hurdle, rather than depleting me, added something. A layer of capability. A slightly deeper knowledge of what I was capable of. A slightly firmer trust in the voice that had travelled with me from every place I had ever had to leave.

> *Aatha used to say, without ever saying it in so many words, that a person who knows their own strength does not need to be afraid of the unfamiliar. The unfamiliar is simply the familiar that has not yet been met. You walk toward it the same way you walk toward everything else — with your full attention, your complete presence, and the quiet certainty that you have everything you need, because the people who shaped you made sure of it.*

I did not fully understand this when she was alive. I understand it now — in every new room I walk into, in every stranger I approach without fear, in every moment I find myself equal to a situation I did not expect. That is her. That is him. Still travelling with me, through every door I open, into every country I arrive in alone.

Chapter – 18 – Everyone is good in their own way

Not every friendship needs a daily greeting.
Not every bond needs to be maintained
like a machine that stops working
the moment you stop feeding it.
Some friendships simply exist —
deep, quiet, available —
whenever they are truly needed.

I have many friends. Across cities, across countries, across the various chapters of a life that has moved often and settled in many different places. And if you were to look at my phone on any given morning, you would not find a trail of good morning messages sent and received, no chain of daily check-ins, no stream of forwarded quotes to prove that someone is thinking of you. That is simply not the register in which my friendships operate.

For a long time, I wondered if this made me a poor friend. Whether the absence of the daily gesture — the morning greeting, the evening check-in, the small digital acknowledgement that you exist and are thought of — was a failure of care. Whether people would drift, would feel neglected, would conclude that the silence meant indifference.

What I discovered, over time, is that the friendships worth keeping do not require that kind of maintenance. The people who truly know you understand, without needing it explained, that your silence is not absence. That you are there — completely, reliably, with your full attention — the moment something real requires you. And they learned this not because I told them but because the times I showed up proved it.

When something actually happened — when the conflict arose, when the pressure mounted, when the situation required someone who would listen without judgment and speak without agenda — they called. And I was there. That is the only currency that matters in a friendship of any real depth. Not the daily greeting. The presence when presence is needed.

I will be honest about something. In the earlier years, when a friend called with a problem, I did not always begin by listening. I joined. I matched their energy, added my own heat to theirs, spoke up with the confidence of someone who already knew what needed to be said before the full story had been told. It felt, at the time, like solidarity. Like being on their side.

But solidarity that speaks before it listens is not always useful. Sometimes it adds noise to a situation that needs quiet. Sometimes the person on the other end of the call does not need someone to be outraged alongside them. They need someone to receive the full weight of what they are carrying before offering anything in return.

I learned this the slow way — through the moments when my early speaking did not help, when the conversation ended and the person on the other end seemed no lighter than before. I began to listen differently. To let the whole story arrive before I reached for a response. And what I found, in that fuller listening, was that the response that was actually needed was rarely the dramatic one. It was almost always the simple one.

> *"Nothing happened. You go. I am always here — whenever you need, however you need, for as long as you need."*

Those words, said with genuine meaning after genuine listening, did more than any speech I had given in the years before. They did not solve the problem. They gave the person permission to stand back up. To believe that the difficulty was survivable. To feel, in the most practical sense, that they were not alone in it. And from that place — feeling held rather than advised — they found their own way through.

I recognised, in this, something Aatha had always done. She never rushed to the answer. She let the person finish. She received what was being offered and then responded to what was actually there — not to what she had expected to hear, not to a version of the problem she had already decided how to solve. She listened first and completely. Then she spoke. And when she spoke, it landed.

My own conflicts I have largely handled alone. Not because I am closed or because I distrust the people around me, but because I learned early that waiting for someone else to fix your situation is a form of standing still. You can speak about a difficulty, share it, be heard in it — and these things have value. But the changing of it is yours to do. No one else can do it for you, and expecting them to is a way of giving your power away.

So I handled things. One at a time, in my own way, with the specific combination of stubbornness and adaptability that I did not choose but seem to have been given. When the situation called for a loud step, I made it loud. When it called for a quieter one, I found the quiet. When I made things worse — and I did, sometimes, push too hard or hold too firm when a different approach would have served better — I let the worse outcome teach me. I changed the perspective. I recalibrated. I did not stay in the worse place and call it the only place.

This is not a story about never needing anyone. It is a story about knowing the difference between what you need to carry alone and what you need to share. Some things are yours to carry. Not because no one would help, but because the carrying of them is itself the growth. The muscle is built by the weight, not by having the weight removed.

Appachi understood this. He never intervened in a difficulty he could see me working through on my own if the working through was what was needed. He watched, and he was available, and he trusted the process. That trust — the trust that you are capable of arriving at your own answer — is its own form of support. Sometimes the most supportive thing a person can do is simply believe in you and wait.

There was a time when I talked to people — made conversation, extended myself, was present in social situations — partly from genuine interest and partly from the quieter, less acknowledged motivation of proving something. Proving that I was capable. That I was good. That I belonged in the rooms I found myself in. That the person standing here was someone worth knowing.

It is an exhausting way to move through the world. The performance of competence is far more tiring than actual competence, because actual competence has the confidence to simply do the thing and let the doing speak. Performance requires constant monitoring — of how you are being received, of whether the impression is landing, of what the next move should be to maintain the image you are trying to project.

The shift came gradually. Not in a single moment of revelation but in the slow accumulation of enough experience to finally see clearly. Everyone is good in their own way. Every person in every room has something that is genuinely theirs — a knowledge, a perspective, a quality of attention, a way of being in the world that no one else possesses in quite the same form. The person I was trying to impress was impressive in their own right. The room I was trying to belong to already contained people who belonged to it differently than I did, and my way of belonging was no less valid than theirs.

When I stopped needing to prove and started simply doing my work — the actual work, the chess coaching, the teaching, the genuine engagement with the people in front of me — something relaxed. Not in my effort, which remained as full as it had ever been. But in the quality of the effort. It became cleaner. Less weighted with self-consciousness. More directed at the actual purpose.

> *Do your work. That is the core. Not the impression of work, not the appearance of competence, not the performance of belonging. Simply the work itself, done with full attention, for the people it is meant to serve. Everything else follows from that, or it does not need to follow at all.*

Aatha never explained this to me. She simply lived it. She did her work — the baskets, the embroidery, the listening, the guiding — without requiring anyone to confirm that the work was valuable. Its value was self-evident to anyone who received it. She did not need the room to applaud her. She needed the work to be well done.

I am still learning to hold that standard for myself. Some days I hold it better than others. But it is the direction. And the direction, as Appachi always understood, is more important than the pace. If you are moving toward the right thing, even slowly, you will arrive.

Chapter – 19 – Show them, don't tell them

A child is not listening to your instructions.
A child is watching your life.
Everything you say they should be,
they are quietly checking
against everything you are.

We tell our children to be perfect. Not in those exact words, perhaps, but in the accumulation of a hundred daily corrections: don't shout, talk politely, give respect to elders, walk properly, don't jump on the furniture, say thank you, say sorry, sit still, pay attention. The instructions arrive in a continuous stream, well-intentioned and entirely sincere, from parents who genuinely want to give their children the best possible version of themselves.

And yet the instructions, so carefully delivered, so consistently repeated, so firmly meant — do not always land. The child continues to shout. Continues to be impolite. Continues to jump. And the parent, bewildered and frustrated, repeats the instruction louder, firmer, with more emphasis, as though the problem were volume or clarity rather than something more fundamental.

The something more fundamental is this: children do not learn from what we say. They learn from what we do. Not occasionally, not in the moments when we remember to perform our values for an audience, but in the ordinary unrehearsed moments of daily life — the moments when we think no one important is watching, when we believe the child is occupied elsewhere, when we have forgotten that the small person in the room is absorbing everything with an attention that shames most adults.

If we speak politely, they will speak politely. Not because we told them to, but because polite speech is the water they swim in, the air they breathe, the only register of conversation they have ever witnessed at close range. If we give respect — to elders, to strangers, to the person who delivers our food, to the child themselves — they will give respect, because respect is what they understand a person to be. If we say sorry when we are wrong and thank you when we are served, those words will live in them as naturally as their own names.

> *We do not teach children values by announcing them. We transmit values by living them — completely, consistently, in the thousand small moments that make up an ordinary day.*

Consider the child who is asked to study while the adult beside them scrolls through a device. The instruction is clear: this is study time, this is important, your future depends on your attention to this book. The instruction is sincere. And yet the message the child receives is different from the message the adult intends to send. What the child sees is an adult who has decided that their own screen is more interesting than the child's education. What the child learns is not the value of study but the value of the screen.

We cannot ask of children what we are unwilling to ask of ourselves. This is not a comfortable truth. It requires us to look honestly at what we are modelling in the moments we are not paying attention to what we are modelling. It requires us to sit with the child, open our own book, and study alongside them — not as a performance of virtue but as a genuine act of shared effort. When the child sees the adult also working, also applying themselves, also treating the time as something worth taking seriously, the message that lands is entirely different. Study is not punishment. Study is what serious people do. And the adult at the table is a serious person.

This is what Aatha and Appachi did, though they would never have described it in these terms. They did not instruct me to read. They read. They did not tell me that learning was valuable. They learned — from books, from conversations, from the Warli art on a hotel wall, from every piece of the world that came within their attention. They treated knowledge as a living thing, something to be actively pursued rather than passively received, and in doing so they made me want to pursue it too. Not because they told me to. Because they showed me what it looked like in a person, and I wanted to look like that.

There is something that happens in certain homes, at certain gatherings, in certain conversations between adults where children are present — something so common that it has stopped being noticed as what it actually is. A parent makes a joke at the child's expense. Points out a weakness or a failure in front of others, with a laugh, in the tone of someone sharing an amusing anecdote. The adults smile. The child smiles too, because the child has learned that this is what is expected in this situation. But something registers. Something is recorded.

Children are not blank. They feel the weight of being exposed in front of others. They feel the particular shame of having their inadequacy offered as entertainment. And what they learn from this — the thing they carry forward without knowing they are carrying it — is that this is how people treat the ones they are closest to. This is what love looks like when it is not being careful. And one day, in their own friendships and their own families, they will do the same thing, without knowing they learned it, without being able to trace it back to the afternoon someone laughed at them in a room full of people.

Protect the dignity of your child in public. Not because children are fragile — they are, in many ways, far more resilient than we give them credit for. But because the habits of how we speak about and to the people we love are formed early and last long. What you practise in the small moments becomes what you do in the large ones. And the child who is never diminished in front of others grows into an adult who does not diminish the people they love.

The most effective thing we can do for a child is not to instruct them but to work alongside them. Not to order the task but to share it. Not to stand above and direct but to sit beside and do.

This is harder. Standing above and directing is efficient. It gets the task done, the child learns the procedure, the outcome is achieved. But something essential is missing from this kind of learning: the experience of effort shared. The knowledge that the adult finds the task worth doing too. The warmth of having been invited into something rather than assigned to it.

Aatha never said: go and make the basket. She said: let us make it together. And in that together, everything was different. The task became a shared world. The skill transferred not as instruction but as participation. And the day we carried those baskets to school with pride, the pride was real — not the pride of having completed an assignment but the pride of having made something with our own hands in the company of someone we loved.

Sit with them. Do with them. Let them see you struggle with something and work through it. Let them see you make a mistake and correct it without drama. Let them see you ask a question because you genuinely do not know the answer. These moments — the unguarded, imperfect, fully human moments — are more educational than any formal lesson, because they show the child not a perfect model to be imitated but a real person to be accompanied.

When I was small, writing a greeting note was genuinely difficult for me. The words did not come easily. The form felt foreign, the expectation unclear. I struggled with it in the way children struggle with things that are slightly beyond their current reach. It did not feel, at the time, like the beginning of anything.

Today, I have written a book.

Not because someone sat me down at the right age and taught me the mechanics of writing. But because people around me treated language as something alive and worth engaging with. Because they read in front of me and discussed what they read. Because they told stories in the evenings and received stories with genuine attention. Because the environment I grew up in was one in which words mattered, and that environment did its slow, invisible work on me over years until one day I found that I had things to say and, more than that, a way to say them.

Children are trees. We are planting the seed when they are small and we are giving them everything they need to grow — the water of our attention, the light of our example, the soil of a home that is arranged around things that matter. We will not always see the fruit. Sometimes the tree grows slowly. Sometimes it takes a direction we did not expect. Sometimes the fruit appears long after we thought the season had passed, for people we will never meet, in circumstances we could not have imagined.

This is not a reason to plant less carefully. It is the reason to plant more carefully. Because the tree will outlast the planting. What we put into the ground today will be living long after we are gone, offering shade and fruit to people who may never know our names but will be shaped, nonetheless, by the quality of what we grew.

> *Aatha and Appachi did not tell me who to be. They grew me — in the particular soil of their daily lives, with the specific nutrients of their attention and their example and their patient, consistent presence. I am the tree they planted. And everything I am able to offer to the world — every student I encourage, every person I support, every morning I begin with intention — is fruit from their planting.*

Let us grow our children the same way. Not through the force of our instructions but through the example of our living. Not by demanding their perfection but by practising our own, imperfectly and honestly, in full view of the small people who are watching everything.

Be the tree. In all weathers — the cyclone and the calm, the summer heat and the monsoon rain. Stand. Do your work. Let your roots hold. The fruit will come.

Chapter – 20 – The world record I already held

The mornings we had as children
were not missing anything.
We did not know this then.
We were too busy living inside them
to understand what they were worth.

Most mornings now begin before they are ready to be begun. I am running before the day has fully arrived — coffee missed or swallowed quickly standing at the counter, the mind already three steps ahead of the body, already sorting through the list that never quite empties. This task. That payment. The grocery order. The vegetables. The investment due. The commitment made last week that arrives this week with its full weight. Each item reasonable on its own, each one legitimate, the whole accumulation forming a kind of permanent background hum that is the soundtrack of a life being managed rather than lived.

I am not complaining. This is the life I have built and it is a good one. But some mornings, in the brief gap between one task and the next, something surfaces — a smell, a quality of light, a specific texture of quietness — and for a moment I am somewhere else entirely. In a house where the morning had a completely different character. Where busy meant something different. Where the day's work was done not in front of a screen or behind a deadline but with hands and sunlight and the particular unhurried effort of people who were making things rather than managing them.

Those mornings were also busy. Make no mistake about that. Aatha's hands were never still. The kitchen was always in motion, always producing something — not just the meals of the day but the preserved, prepared, carefully made things that would last for weeks or months. Pickles that required exact ratios of salt and spice and the patience to let time do its work. Papad laid out in precise rows, each one evenly thin, set to dry in the particular morning sun that Aatha seemed to understand the way a farmer understands their land — knowing its quality, its direction, its moods.

The balcony was its own small world during these seasons. Sun-dried vegetables spread out on woven trays, drying slowly in the heat, requiring monitoring and turning and protection. Protection from the birds that arrived with their own clear opinions about what belonged to whom. Protection from the squirrels that treated every unattended tray as a personal invitation. And occasionally — this memory makes me smile every time it surfaces — protection from us. The children. Who were themselves a kind of weather, unpredictable and enthusiastic and not always careful about what they disturbed in the course of being nine years old.

Appachi presided over some of this with the calm authority of a man who understood that a household running well is not an accident but a practice. He was the chef of the family in the way that certain people are the centre of a thing without needing to announce it — not by standing at the stove at every meal, but by being the person around whom the kitchen organised itself, whose preferences shaped the menu, whose presence at the table made the meal feel complete.

We helped. Not because we were assigned roles but because the work was happening and we were there and being included felt better than being outside it. We fetched things. We held things. We were sent on small errands to relatives and friends, carrying parcels of pickle and papad with the seriousness of people entrusted with something important — which, in the economy of that house, we were. These deliveries were not logistics. They were the physical form of connection — the household saying to the people around it: we made something good and we want you to have some.

For each piece of work we did, we received a small payment. Not a large amount — the kind of amount that a child can hold in one hand and still feel rich. It went into a box. A proper box, with a lid, kept somewhere specific, which gave the saving a weight and a location that a digital balance could never quite replicate. You could hear the money in the box when you lifted it. You could feel it growing, coin by coin, task by task, over days and weeks of small efforts accumulating into something that had not existed before.

When enough had gathered, we spent it. Not on devices, not on the things that require a charger and a screen and a monthly subscription. On story books, mostly. Small paperback worlds that could be held in both hands and carried everywhere and read in the particular absorbed way of a child who has purchased the thing themselves and therefore owns it in a way that goes beyond the legal. The ownership was emotional. It was earned. And the story inside the book arrived differently because of that — received with a quality of attention and gratitude that things given freely do not always receive.

The day I walked home with one of those books, chosen carefully from the shelf with the coins I had saved from weeks of balcony-watching and parcel-carrying and pickle-helping, I felt something that I did not have a name for then and can only approximately name now. It was the feeling of having done something in the world and been met with a real result. Of effort and outcome being directly, visibly, holdably connected. Of being, in the small but entirely genuine economy of a child's life, someone who had accomplished something.

> *I felt, in that moment, like I had set a world record. Not in anything that would be measured or recorded or reported. Simply in the private, uncomplicated register of a child who has worked for something and received it and stands in the afternoon light holding the proof.*

And then there was everything outside. The street, which was its own complete universe. Street cricket played with improvised equipment on improvised pitches, the rules adjusted to suit the available space and the available players, the game entirely serious within its own invented framework. Hide and seek in the particular geography of a neighbourhood that had been mapped, over hundreds of games, into a complete taxonomy of hiding places — which ones were known, which ones were still secret, which ones had been discovered and abandoned and rediscovered by the next generation of players.

The jumps from one wall to the next, from one balcony ledge to another, with the complete physical confidence of children who have not yet learned to be afraid of heights because no one has yet told them convincingly enough that they should be. The scraped knees and the dust on the uniform and the return home slightly later than stated, slightly more dishevelled than expected, carrying the evidence of an afternoon fully spent.

The bunked classes. I will not pretend these did not happen, because they did, and because they belong honestly to the texture of a 90s childhood in a way that no accounting of that time can leave out without falsifying it. The collaboration required. The alibi constructed. The specific thrill of a Tuesday afternoon that was supposed to be in a classroom but was instead somewhere else entirely, doing something that required no permission and left no record except in memory, which has kept it faithfully.

These things — the cricket, the hiding, the jumping, the occasional strategic absence from school — were not the interruptions of childhood. They were its substance. The unscheduled, unmonitored, genuinely free hours in which children discover what they are when no adult is directing them. What they enjoy. What they are brave enough to attempt. What they will risk for the company of friends. What the world feels like when it belongs to you for an afternoon.

When I look back at all of this now — from the distance of years and countries and the particular vantage point of someone who has learned, the hard way, what an unhurried morning is worth — I see what I could not see while I was inside it. I see a childhood that was rich in exactly the things that matter and simple in exactly the ways that serve a person for life. Not wealthy by any external measure. Not equipped with the devices and entertainments and optimised learning environments that we now consider essential to a proper upbringing. But full. Genuinely, completely full.

Full of people who were present. Full of work that was shared. Full of food that was made rather than ordered. Full of mornings that began before the sun and used the light completely. Full of the specific, irreplaceable education of being included in the real work of a real household by real people who trusted you enough to give you a role in it.

The world record I held then was not measured in any category that appears in any record book. It was measured in the quality of the ordinary days. In the smell of pickle being prepared and the sound of coins in a box and the weight of a paperback bought with saved money and the feeling of sun on the balcony while the vegetables dried and the birds watched and the squirrels plotted and the morning moved at exactly the pace a morning should move.

Today, when I miss a coffee and run past the grocery list and manage the payments and plan the investments, I sometimes stop. Just for a moment. Just long enough to hear, somewhere underneath the hum of the managed life, the echo of a different kind of morning. The kind that asked nothing of you except your presence. The kind that gave you everything it had, simply because you were there.

> *Aatha and Appachi gave me those mornings. Every single one. They gave them without knowing they were giving anything remarkable, because to them it was simply life — the ordinary, unhurried, fully inhabited life of two people who understood, without ever putting it into words, that the quality of the days is the quality of the life. That the ordinary*

morning, lived with full attention and shared with genuine warmth, is not the backdrop to something more important. It is the most important thing there is.

I am still learning to live that way. Still reaching, across the distance of years and busyness, toward the mornings they made. Still finding, in the best of my days, something that carries their quality — a slowness, a fullness, a sense of being exactly where I am supposed to be, doing exactly what I am supposed to be doing, with nothing missing.

Those mornings were the world record. I just did not know it yet.

Epilogue

What We Leave Behind

The greatest inheritance
is not something kept in a locker
or written in a document.
It is something kept in a person —
in the way they stand after falling,
in the way they face what comes,
in the quiet certainty
that they are enough.

We work hard for the people who come after us. We save, we build, we accumulate — property, gold, the various forms of material security that a responsible generation leaves for the next. These things have value. I do not dismiss them. But they are not the most important thing we leave behind. They are not the thing that will determine whether the person who receives them is capable of standing on their own ground, facing an uncertain world, and moving through it with clarity and strength.

The most important thing we leave behind cannot be stored. It cannot be locked away or insured or transferred through a legal document. It lives in the person we have shaped — in their relationship with failure, in their capacity for patience, in their willingness to get back up after a fall with more understanding than they had before the fall. In the quiet, unshakeable knowledge that difficulty is not the end. That the comeback is always possible. That the comeback, in fact, is where the real formation happens.

If the next generation inherits property but no resilience, they will lose the property. If they inherit gold but no values, the gold will not save them from the moments that require something gold cannot buy. But if they inherit the knowledge of how to stand — how to fall and rise, how to lose and continue, how to face the unfamiliar without being undone by it — then they carry something that no circumstance can take from them. That is the asset that compounds across generations. That is the inheritance worth building.

Let them fall. Let them feel the ground. And then be there — not to carry them, but to remind them that they already have what they need to rise. The comeback has to be stronger than the fall. That is not a consolation. That is the whole teaching.

I do not know whether I will become what Aatha and Appachi were. I do not know whether I carry their wisdom with the same effortless consistency, the same daily faithfulness, the same complete absence of performance that made their lives so quietly extraordinary. Some days I come closer than others. Some days I fall short in ways I recognise only in retrospect, when I look back at the day and see the moment I could have been patient and was not, the moment I could have listened and spoke too soon.

But I carry the direction. I carry the knowledge of what it looked like when it was done right. I carry twenty years of watching two people live with a quality of presence and intention and genuine warmth that I have not encountered at the same level anywhere else, in anyone else, in all the years and places since. That is not nothing. That is, in fact, everything. Because you cannot move toward something you have never seen. They showed me what it looks like. The rest is the work of a lifetime.

I will try to be there for the next generation in my own way, with their resemblance. Not as a copy — I am not them, and the world they will inherit is not the world in which Aatha and Appachi built their lives. But in the essential things: in the quality of presence I bring to the people I love. In the willingness to sit beside rather than stand above. In the belief that every person is capable of more than they currently know, and that the most powerful thing you can do for someone is to hold that belief steadily, even when they cannot hold it for themselves.

If you have read this far, you have spent time with two people who never sought an audience. Aatha and Appachi did not live the way they lived in order to be written about. They lived that way because it was, to them, simply the right way to live — with care, with consistency, with the daily unremarkable faithfulness of people who have decided what matters and organised their lives around it without requiring the world to notice.

I hope this book has returned you, at least briefly, to someone in your own life who shaped you in the quiet way. The person whose presence you took for granted because it was so constant, so reliable, so entirely woven into the fabric of your ordinary days that you did not see it as a gift until it was no longer there. Or perhaps they are still there — still present, still doing their patient, invisible work of holding you and shaping you — and this book has been an invitation to look at them more clearly. To say, while you still can, what you may have left unsaid.

Whatever you carry from these pages, I hope it is this: the ordinary days are not the backdrop to your life. They are your life. The morning coffee. The shared meal. The small correction given with patience instead of anger. The walk taken without a destination. The conversation that goes wherever it goes. These things, repeated across years with genuine attention and genuine love, are the most powerful force of formation available to any human being. Not the grand gestures. Not the large investments. The ordinary days, lived well, with the people who matter, fully present to what is actually happening.

> *Do your work. Be the tree. Show them, don't tell them. Keep the pain in its corner and the smile outside. Listen before you speak. And when you fall — because you will fall — let the comeback be stronger.*

That is what they gave me. That is what I am trying to give forward. That is what I hope, in your own way, in your own house, with your own people, you will find a way to give too.

To Aatha and Appachi —

Thank you for the mornings.

Thank you for the coffee I begged for and received in small amounts.

Thank you for the one question that was better than a hundred lectures.

Thank you for the railway platform and the Warli art and the banana leaf parcels.

Thank you for letting me fall and trusting me to rise.

Thank you for never telling me who to be —

and for showing me, every single day, what a person can be.

I am still becoming you.
And I always will be.

— Valli Saran